The Essential Golf Cart Buyer's Handbook

Avoid Getting Ripped Off

H.S. Collins

Copyright © 2025 H.S. Collins

All rights reserved.

No part of this book may be used or reproduced, distributed, or transmitted in any form or by any means, including photocopying, recording, or other electronic or mechanical methods, without the proper written permission of the publisher, except in the case of brief quotations apart, embodied in critical reviews and certain other non-commercial uses permitted by copyright law. Use of this publication is permitted solely for personal use and must include full attribution of the material's source.

NO AI TRAINING: Without in any way limiting the author's exclusive rights under copyright, any use of this publication to "train" generative artificial intelligence (AI) technologies to generate text is expressly prohibited. The author reserves all rights to license uses of this work for generative AI training and development of machine learning language models.

Ebook ISBN: 979-8-9929146-0-3

Paperback ISBN: 979-8-9929146-1-0

Table of Contents

Introduction 5

Chapter 1: Why a Golf Cart, and Why This Handbook? 6

Chapter 2: Golf Cart Basics – Types, Uses, and Key Components 9

Chapter 3: Gas vs. Electric Golf Carts – Which is Right for You? 15

Chapter 4: Understanding Batteries and Power in Electric Carts 22

Chapter 5: New vs. Used Golf Carts – Pros, Cons, and Considerations 30

Chapter 6: Where to Buy – Dealerships, Private Sellers, and Online Marketplaces 38

Chapter 7: Key Features and Specifications to Evaluate 47

Chapter 8: Major Golf Cart Brands and Models – A Buyer's Overview 55

Chapter 9: Customization and Accessories – Making the Cart Your Own 64

Chapter 10: Street Legal and Regulatory Considerations 73

Chapter 11: Maintenance and Upkeep – Keeping Your Cart Running Smoothly 82

Chapter 12: Operating Costs and Budgeting for Ownership 94

Chapter 13: The Buying Process – Step-by-Step and Checklist 105

Chapter 14: Conclusion and Future Trends 117

About the Author 125

Introduction

WELCOME TO *The Essential Golf Cart Buyer's Handbook*, your comprehensive guide to navigating the world of golf carts. Whether you're a golfer looking for personal transportation on the course, a homeowner in a cart-friendly community, or a business seeking efficient utility vehicles, this handbook will equip you with expert insights and in-depth knowledge. We'll cover everything from the basics of golf cart types and key features to deep dives on electric vs. gas models, maintenance, customization, legal considerations, and beyond. By the end, you'll be well-prepared to make an informed purchase and enjoy years of smooth rides.

Chapter 1:
Why a Golf Cart, and Why This Handbook?

BUYING A GOLF CART is an exciting venture, but it can also be a significant investment. Today's golf carts aren't just for golfers – they've evolved into multi-purpose vehicles popular in retirement communities, college campuses, farms, warehouses, and neighborhoods. In some communities, residents use golf carts to run errands or visit friends nearby as a convenient, eco-friendly alternative to cars. This handbook exists to guide you through the *entire* buying process, ensuring you get the right cart for your needs and budget.

Golf carts (often simply called "carts," even though the original term was "golf car") have come a long way. Originally, a "golf cart" referred to a pull-cart for clubs or a small two-seater electric car for the course. Over time, the term has expanded to cover

The Essential Golf Cart Buyer's Handbook

any small motorized vehicle used on golf courses or for short-distance travel. What was once just a way to shuttle golfers and their bags has become a **versatile personal vehicle** category. Modern golf carts can carry multiple passengers, haul cargo, and even drive on public streets in some cases.

A typical two-seater golf cart on the course, designed to carry golfers and their equipment around 18 holes. Modern carts like this are the starting point for many buyers, offering simplicity and reliability for golfing needs.

Why consider a golf cart? For one, they're fun and practical. They provide quick, easy transportation for short trips without the expense and hassle of a full-sized car. They're also relatively easy to maintain, and electric models produce no emissions and very little noise – a big plus for environmentally conscious buyers or those who enjoy peaceful drives. Golf carts have become a fixture in many gated and retirement communities because they strike a perfect balance between convenience and cost-effectiveness. They allow older adults or anyone who prefers not to drive a car to maintain mobility and independence within their community.

However, buying a golf cart is not as simple as picking the first one you see. There's a wide range of options: **new vs. used, gas vs. electric, two-seater**

vs. six-seater, basic vs. fully loaded. Prices can vary from a couple of thousand dollars for a used cart to well over $10,000 for a new, feature-rich model. As with automobiles, you'll need to consider your specific needs, compare features, and understand maintenance and legal responsibilities. That's where this handbook comes in – to break down all those factors into digestible, expert-backed guidance.

Throughout this eBook, we'll provide **expert insights, research, checklists, and illustrations** to help you each step of the way. Our goal is to make the content reader-friendly yet authoritative. If you're a first-time buyer, this guide will answer your pressing questions and maybe some you didn't know to ask. If you're an experienced owner looking for an upgrade, you'll find up-to-date info on the latest trends like lithium batteries and street-legal carts. Let's embark on this journey to find *your* perfect golf cart!

Chapter 2:
Golf Cart Basics – Types, Uses, and Key Components

BEFORE DIVING INTO purchase decisions, it's important to understand the basics of golf carts – what types are available and how they're built. A golf cart (or "golf car" in technical terms) is essentially a *small motorized vehicle originally designed to carry golfers and equipment* around a course. Nowadays, these carts come in various configurations and are used far beyond the golf course.

Common Types of Golf Carts by Use:
- **Golf Course Carts:** These are the standard two-seater electric or gas carts you see at golf courses. They typically have simple bench seating for two, a spot for two golf bags in the back, and a top speed of around 15-20 mph.

They prioritize smooth acceleration and turf-friendly tires to avoid damaging greens.
- **Personal Transportation Vehicles (PTVs):** Often used in communities or large properties, PTVs might have 2 to 6 seats and often come with features like lights, turn signals, and storage options. They're designed for neighborhoods, retirement communities, resorts, and similar settings where residents drive on local streets or pathways.
- **Utility and Off-Road Carts:** Some carts are built or modified for utility work – for example, with a cargo bed for hauling landscaping tools, feed on a farm, or equipment in a warehouse. Off-road variants might have lifted suspensions, all-terrain tires, and more powerful motors or engines to handle trails and rough terrain.
- **Commercial and Specialty Carts:** Many businesses use golf carts or "utility vehicles" for specific purposes – airports and malls use them for maintenance or security patrols, parks use them for ranger vehicles, and large campuses use them for transportation. Some carts are modified as shuttles, food trucks, or even mobile workshops.
- **Low-Speed Vehicles (LSVs):** These are beefed-up carts (often electric) that meet

certain federal requirements to be street legal (more on this in Chapter 9). They usually have additional safety features (lights, mirrors, seat belts, etc.) and can travel on public roads with speed limits up to 35 mph.

Beyond use-case categories, golf carts can be categorized by their **power source** and **design features**, which we'll explore in upcoming chapters. It's also useful to know the key components that make up a golf cart:

- **Chassis and Frame:** The frame is the structural backbone. Many carts use steel frames, but some premium brands like Club Car use rust-proof aluminum frames which are lighter and resist corrosion.
- **Drivetrain:** This includes either an electric motor (powered by batteries) or a gasoline engine, plus the transmission or gearing that drives the wheels. Electric carts often have a direct-drive or simple gear differential (no multi-gear transmission like a car). Gas carts have small engines (around 10-15 horsepower) and sometimes a continuously variable transmission (CVT).
- **Battery Pack (for Electric Carts):** Electric models have multiple deep-cycle batteries (usually 36-volt or 48-volt systems comprised of 6V, 8V, or 12V batteries in

series – we'll discuss this more in Chapter 4). The batteries are the fuel tank of an electric cart, providing the energy to the motor.
- **Fuel System (for Gas Carts):** In gas-powered carts, instead of batteries you'll have a small gasoline tank (usually 5-6 gallon capacity) feeding the engine. Modern gas carts may have 4-stroke engines similar to those in small cars or utility ATVs.
- **Controller and Electronics:** In electric carts, a speed controller regulates the power from the batteries to the motor, controlling acceleration and speed. Both electric and gas carts have wiring for lights, horn, ignition, etc., and many have onboard computers or regulators for charging or governing speed.
- **Steering and Suspension:** Carts use a simpler version of automotive steering (often rack-and-pinon or steering box) and have basic suspension – usually independent suspension in front and leaf springs in the rear. High-end or newer models might have improved independent suspension for a smoother ride.
- **Brakes:** Most carts have mechanical drum brakes on the rear wheels (and sometimes front brakes on faster models or LSVs). Some electric carts also have regenerative braking via the motor, which helps slow the cart and

recharge the battery slightly when going downhill.
- **Body and Seats:** The bodies are often made of molded plastic or fiberglass. They can be basic or styled to look sporty or like mini-cars. Seats range from simple vinyl-covered bench seats to plush, upholstered seats with armrests in luxury models.
- **Tires and Wheels:** Standard golf course carts have small turf tires (18-inch diameter or so) that are smooth. Off-road or street carts might have larger, knobbier tires or street tread and stylish wheels. Wheel size and type can affect ride comfort and clearance.
- **Accessories:** Many carts come with or can be fitted with windshields, roofs, side mirrors, turn signals, headlights/taillights, and other accessories like ball holders, coolers, GPS holders, and more.

Understanding these basics will help you communicate with dealers or sellers and grasp why certain features matter. For instance, knowing that an electric cart's performance heavily depends on its **battery pack and controller** will make Chapter 4 (on batteries) even more relevant. Likewise, recognizing that a cart's frame material can affect durability (steel vs. aluminum) might influence your brand choices in Chapter 8.

In the next chapter, we'll tackle one of the biggest decisions you'll face: choosing between a **gas-powered** cart and an **electric** one. This choice impacts everything from daily convenience to long-term maintenance and costs, so it's crucial to weigh the pros and cons carefully.

Chapter 3:
Gas vs. Electric Golf Carts – Which is Right for You?

ONE OF THE MOST fundamental choices when buying a golf cart is deciding between a gas-powered cart and an electric cart. Each type has its own advantages and drawbacks, and the best choice depends on how you plan to use the cart. Let's break down the **pros and cons** of gas vs. electric golf carts, as well as key considerations like power, range, and maintenance for each.

Power and Performance: Gas carts are typically equipped with small gasoline engines (often single-cylinder, 4-stroke engines similar to those in riding lawnmowers or small ATVs). They generally have higher horsepower than electric motors, which can translate to better performance in certain situations – for example, climbing steep hills or carrying heavy loads. Gas carts can often handle *longer distances* or continuous use because you can refill the gas tank quickly and keep going. On the other hand, electric carts have **instant torque** from their electric motors, meaning they accelerate smoothly and quickly (no engine rev-up needed). Many owners appreciate that an electric cart's acceleration is almost immediate and power delivery is very smooth. For flat terrain and typical loads, electrics have plenty of pep; and some high-end electric models can reach top speeds of 20–25 mph, rivaling or exceeding gas carts in speed.

Range and Refuel/Recharge: With a gas cart, range anxiety is minimal – if the tank is full, you might go 100+ miles, and if you run low, a 5-minute stop at a gas can or station gets you back to full. Electric carts run on batteries, so their range is limited by battery capacity. Most electric golf carts can handle **18 to 36 holes of golf (roughly 6-15 miles) on a full charge**, and newer models with lithium batteries can often go even further. Recharging an electric cart typically takes several hours (6-8 hours for a full charge from empty, usually done overnight). So, if you plan to use a cart for an extended day of driving (such as a full day at a large outdoor event or an all-day work shift), a gas cart might be more convenient unless you have a way to recharge or swap batteries midday. However, for the average homeowner or golfer using the cart intermittently, an electric cart's range is usually sufficient.

Operating Cost: Electricity is almost always cheaper than gasoline on a per-mile basis. Charging an electric cart's batteries might only cost a few cents per mile (depending on local electricity rates), whereas buying gas is more expensive per mile driven. According to some comparisons, **electric golf carts are notably less costly to operate and maintain than gas carts** – you don't pay for gas or frequent engine service. Over time, these savings can add up. Gas carts also require oil changes, spark plugs, filters, etc., which we'll discuss in maintenance. Electric carts will eventually need new batteries (every 5-7 years for lead-acid batteries typically), which is a significant expense but infrequent.

Noise and Environment: Here electric carts win hands-down. Electric carts run almost silently and produce **zero tailpipe emissions**. If you cruise around a quiet community or on a peaceful morning golf round, the lack of engine noise is a big plus – you can even hold a conversation without raising your voice. Gas carts, in contrast, make engine noise (newer ones are quieter than old two-stroke engines from decades past, but they still buzz and hum). Gas engines also emit exhaust fumes. On a golf course or nature preserve, the smell and pollution from gas exhaust can be a downside, and some courses or communities **prohibit gas carts** for these reasons. Environmentalists often prefer electric carts as they don't contribute to air pollution on-site.

Convenience and Use Case: Think about how and where you'll use the cart. If you have a short commute around a gated community, an electric cart that you plug in each night is extremely convenient – no trips to the gas station needed, and you'll start every day with a "full tank" (full charge) if you keep it charged. If you have a large property, farm, or need a cart for an extended workday (like maintenance crew usage), a gas cart might be favored since you can quickly refuel and continue working without waiting. Gas carts might also be preferable in very cold climates, as battery performance can drop in low temperatures (though this is usually a minor issue and can be mitigated with proper battery care or newer battery tech).

Pros and Cons Summary: Let's summarize the general pros and cons of each, as commonly cited by experts and owners:

- **Gas Cart Pros:** Typically more powerful and can have higher top speed out-of-the-box (around 19–20 mph for many, versus 15–19 mph electric, though high-end electrics match them). Better for heavy loads and steep

hills (doesn't drain like a battery might on a long incline). Quick to refuel for continuous use. Can be a "safer option" in the sense you won't get stranded with dead batteries if you have fuel.
- **Gas Cart Cons:** Loud engine noise and exhaust smell. Produces emissions (air pollution). Requires regular engine maintenance (oil changes, spark plugs). Fuel cost adds up and is higher than electricity per mile. Often higher initial cost than equivalent electric models. Not allowed in some communities or courses due to noise or pollution restrictions.
- **Electric Cart Pros:** Silent operation and no emissions – eco-friendly and neighbor-friendly. Smoother acceleration (no jerking gears). Lower operating cost (electricity + less maintenance). Less routine maintenance – no oil changes or engine upkeep, just batteries. Often slightly cheaper upfront and widely available used (many fleets sell used electric carts). Can be charged at home easily.
- **Electric Cart Cons:** Limited range per charge – need to monitor battery level. Long recharge time compared to a gas refill. Loses performance as batteries deplete or age (slower speeds if batteries are low). Batteries eventually need replacement which is costly

(several hundred to a couple thousand dollars, depending on type). Not ideal for very hilly terrain or heavy towing unless you have a high-torque model (though some electrics handle hills fine, steep or long grades will drain batteries faster).

A quick comparison chart for reference:

When deciding between gas and electric, consider *where* and *how long* you'll drive, *what you'll carry*, and *your tolerance for maintenance*. If you plan to use the cart strictly on the golf course or around a quiet neighborhood for short trips, an electric cart is often the preferred choice. If you need a workhorse for an acreage, towing, or all-day events, a gas cart might be more practical.

Finally, note that **hybrid models** (like gas engines with electric assist) are very rare in golf carts – most buyers will be choosing one or the other. Some newer carts use propane or have swappable battery packs, but those are niche. For the vast majority of cases, the gas vs electric dichotomy is the main choice.

In the next chapter, we'll delve deeper into the heart of electric carts: their batteries. Understanding battery types, voltages, and care is crucial if you're considering an electric model (or already set on one), so don't skip it even if you lean electric. Conversely, if you're pro-gas, that chapter will help you appreciate what you're avoiding and also cover some emerging tech (like lithium batteries) that could influence the market.

Chapter 4: Understanding Batteries and Power in Electric Carts

IF YOU'RE CONSIDERING an electric golf cart (which many buyers do, given their low maintenance and quiet operation), it's vital to understand the battery system – it's the equivalent of the engine and fuel tank in a gas cart. Even if you're leaning toward a gas cart, this chapter is worthwhile because battery technology is advancing rapidly and could affect resale value and future options.

Battery Basics: Most traditional electric golf carts use **lead-acid deep-cycle batteries**. These are similar to car batteries but designed to provide steady power over a long period (deep discharge) rather than a short burst of starting current. A typical golf cart has multiple batteries wired in series to create the total voltage the motor requires. Common setups are **36-volt systems** (often 6 x 6V batteries) and **48-volt**

systems (either 6 x 8V batteries, or 4 x 12V, or sometimes 8 x 6V in high-capacity setups). Generally, **48V carts have become more common** because they provide more torque and efficiency than older 36V ones. A higher voltage system can deliver the same power while drawing less current (amperage), which means less heat and better efficiency through the controller and motor, and potentially longer run time for the same capacity. In practical terms, a 48V cart will *accelerate a bit faster* and handle hills better than a 36V cart. If you're looking at used carts, you'll find many older models (pre-2000s) are 36V, whereas most mid-2000s and newer are 48V. If performance is a priority, lean toward 48V models or plan to convert (conversion involves replacing the motor, controller, and adding a battery – not trivial).

Battery Capacity and Range: The capacity of a battery pack is measured in amp-hours (Ah) or sometimes in a more abstract "minutes at 75A" rating for golf cart batteries. Essentially, the higher the capacity, the longer the cart can run per charge. Standard lead-acid packs in a 48V cart might be around 150 Ah, giving, for example, perhaps 20-25 miles range on flat ground. If you plan on using your cart for longer rides, consider upgrades or models with higher capacity batteries. Note that driving conditions greatly affect range – lots of hills or high-speed driving will reduce it. Manufacturers often specify how many rounds of golf or miles a cart can go; real-world range can vary, so when testing a cart, ensure it meets your daily needs with a comfortable margin.

Battery Types: Lead-Acid vs. Lithium: A major development in recent years is the introduction of **lithium-ion batteries** for golf carts. Lithium batteries (like those in Tesla cars or smartphones) have higher energy density, meaning more range for less weight. They also do not require the maintenance that lead-acid batteries do (no watering, less concern about discharge level, etc.). Many new high-end carts offer lithium battery options, and there are conversion kits to retrofit older carts with lithium packs. The benefits of lithium are significant: *lighter weight (improves performance), more consistent power output, faster charging, and longer lifespan*. A lithium pack might last 10+ years, whereas lead-acid batteries often need replacement in 4-6 years of regular use. Lithium batteries can also often be charged partially without harm (no memory effect), whereas lead-acid really prefer to be fully recharged after a use cycle. The downsides of lithium? **Cost**. Lithium carts or conversions can add several thousand dollars to the price. Also, very low temperatures can affect lithium performance (though some have heating elements). If your budget allows, lithium-powered carts are fantastic for long-term value and performance. If you're buying used, you'll mostly encounter lead-acid batteries, but keep an eye out – some owners may have upgraded to lithium, which can drastically increase a used cart's value.

Battery Maintenance (Lead-Acid): If you get a cart with the classic lead-acid batteries, you'll need to perform some routine maintenance to maximize their life. This typically includes: **watering the batteries** – checking each battery cell (via the removable caps) and topping up with distilled water periodically. Batteries should be kept clean and dry; corrosion on terminals should be cleaned with a baking soda solution and a wire brush (while wearing proper safety gear). It's important to **charge the cart after each use** (or daily if used regularly) – leaving batteries partly discharged for extended periods can shorten their life. Also, never let a lead-acid pack run completely dead; deep discharge can harm them. Most chargers nowadays are "smart" chargers that will taper off and maintain a float charge once full – these are great because you can plug in the cart and not worry about overcharging. If the cart comes with an older charger, be cautious about leaving it unattended for days. Modern chargers detect when the batteries are full and will only send current when needed, which prolongs battery life and safety.

Battery Replacement Costs: Eventually, batteries need replacement. For a typical 48V cart with 6 batteries, you might spend anywhere from $600 on the low end (budget batteries) to $1,000+ for premium batteries (like Trojan brand, which is well-known for quality). If you have an 8-battery system, costs go up accordingly. Installation is something you can do yourself with basic tools, but it's heavy work (each battery can weigh 50-70 lbs). Keep this future cost in mind when evaluating a used cart: **always ask how old the batteries are** and if possible, verify the manufacture date on them (battery cases often have a date code). A set of fresh batteries is a huge selling point for a used electric cart, whereas a cart with 5-year-old batteries might soon need an expensive swap. As noted earlier, lithium packs cost more – but their lifespan is roughly double or more, and they might not need any maintenance in the interim. A lithium conversion might run $2,000–$3,000, but prices are gradually coming down.

Charging Setup: Ensure you have a suitable place and electrical outlet to charge your cart. Most chargers plug into a standard 110-120V outlet (in North America) and draw around 10-15 amps. That's like running a big appliance. So you'll want an outlet that doesn't have a bunch of other appliances on the same circuit. Typically a garage outlet is fine. Some carts (especially older ones or certain brands) have specific charger plug types – make sure the charger comes with the cart and is compatible. If you buy new, it will. If you buy used, double-check you get the charger unit in the deal, and test that it works. Additionally, charging in a well-ventilated area is recommended because lead-acid batteries can emit a bit of hydrogen gas during charging – usually not an issue in a garage or carport with some airflow, but don't charge in a tiny closed closet. Follow the manufacturer's guidelines on charging; some suggest leaving the charger connected if the cart is stored long-term (the smart charger will kick on occasionally to maintain charge). Others say to top off monthly.

36V vs 48V vs 72V: As mentioned, 48V is common, and 36V mostly found in older carts. There are also some performance models and utility carts that use **72V systems** (typically 9 x 8V batteries, or a lithium equivalent). These carts can have better acceleration and speed, but they are less common and tend to be specialty or high-end models (e.g., certain Polaris or GEM LSVs, or custom builds). A higher voltage system, in theory, gives more power potential, but also requires appropriate high-voltage components. For standard golf cart needs, 48V hits a sweet spot of performance and cost. If you end up with a 36V cart and find it sluggish, know that converting to 48V is possible but involves replacing multiple components. Some enthusiasts do it for the ~30% gain in power and speed, but if you're not keen on such modifications, it may be better to purchase a cart that already meets your performance needs.

Gas Cart "Batteries": Lest we ignore gas carts entirely in this chapter: note that gas carts still have a small 12V battery on board. It's there to start the engine (and run accessories when the engine's off). It's basically a lawnmower or motorcycle battery. These typically last many years and cost maybe $50-$100 to replace when needed. Gas carts also have alternators to keep that battery charged. So gas owners aren't totally free from battery talk – just much less so.

In summary, if you choose an electric cart, **treat the battery as the critical component**. A well-maintained battery pack is like a well-maintained engine – it's central to performance and longevity. If you choose gas, you can skim this, but also watch the electric space; with lithium tech and more efficient motors, electric carts are only getting better. Who knows, you might be tempted to switch in the future as technology evolves.

Now that we've covered powertrains (gas vs electric and battery details), we can move on to the next major decision point: do you buy a **brand new cart**

from a dealer, or do you look for a **used cart** to save money? Each route has its pros and cons, which we'll explore in the next chapter.

Chapter 5:
New vs. Used Golf Carts – Pros, Cons, and Considerations

WHEN IT COMES TO buying a golf cart, one of the first questions is: **Should you buy new or used?** There's no one-size-fits-all answer, as it depends on budget, preferences, and how comfortable you are with maintenance or potential repairs. This chapter will help you weigh the advantages and disadvantages of each option so you can decide what's best for you.

Buying a New Golf Cart:
Pros of New:

- **Reliability and Warranty:** A new golf cart comes fresh from the factory with no wear

The Essential Golf Cart Buyer's Handbook

and tear. It will include a manufacturer's warranty (often 1-3 years, depending on brand) that can cover any early issues. This peace of mind is a big plus – if something breaks prematurely, you aren't on the hook for the repair cost. You're also unlikely to face any maintenance needs (aside from basic things like battery charging or initial oil change on a gas cart) for a while.

- **Latest Technology and Features:** New carts will have the newest features – whether that's improved battery technology (like a lithium option), advanced motor controllers, modern safety features, or nicer convenience features like USB charging ports, LED lighting, better suspension, or infotainment. If having the cutting-edge matters to you, new is the way to get it.
- **Customization at Purchase:** Many dealers allow you to configure a new cart to your liking – you can choose colors, seat material, add accessories (like a roof, windshield, upgraded wheels, etc.) as part of the purchase. This way, you roll off with a cart that fits your needs exactly, rather than inheriting someone else's configuration and then modifying it.
- **Status and Condition:** Let's be honest – there's something nice about *new*. The cart

will be cosmetically perfect, and you get that new-car (or new-cart) smell. If you're buying for a business or as a gift, a shiny new cart has a certain appeal.

Cons of New:

- **Higher Cost:** Just like cars, new golf carts depreciate once sold. You'll pay a premium for being the first owner. A basic new two-seater might start around $6,000-$8,000, and prices go up with more features (some fully loaded or high-performance carts can be $12,000-$15,000 or more, especially 4 or 6 seaters). In comparison, used carts can be found for a fraction of that. If budget is tight, new may simply be out of reach, or it might strain your finances unnecessarily.
- **Initial Depreciation:** The moment you buy new, it becomes "used" in value. If you needed to resell it within a year or two, you'd likely get noticeably less than you paid, even if you kept it in great shape. With used carts, the previous owner has already absorbed that depreciation.
- **Wait Times:** If you're custom-ordering a cart, you might have to wait for it to be built or delivered, especially if it's a popular model or during peak seasons. Some dealers

stock popular models, though, so this isn't always an issue.

Buying a Used Golf Cart:
Pros of Used:

- **Significant Cost Savings:** The biggest draw of used carts is the lower price. You might find a solid used cart for **half the price (or even less) of new**. For example, a 4-year-old electric cart that sold new for $8,000 might be on the market for $4,000–$5,000, depending on condition. This lower purchase price can make owning a cart very accessible.
- **Less Depreciation Worry:** If you buy a used cart at a fair price, you could potentially use it for a couple of years and sell it for close to what you paid (assuming you keep it in similar condition). The value of a well-kept used cart tends to stabilize after the initial depreciation.
- **Budget for Upgrades:** Money saved on the purchase can be used to customize or upgrade the cart to your liking – new wheels, a better sound system, or even a new battery pack. As one expert noted, the savings from buying used might allow for more budget toward customizations and accessories.

- **Wider Selection of Models:** When shopping used, you might find a mix of older models or unique custom builds that aren't available new anymore. This can be good if you have a specific style in mind or if older models had features you prefer. The second-hand market can offer a *wide array of models across many years*, giving you more choices.

Cons of Used:

- **Unknown Condition & History:** A used cart comes with wear and tear. Depending on how it was maintained, it might have issues that aren't immediately obvious. Batteries might be near the end of their life, or a gas engine might need a tune-up. There's also a risk of hidden problems – maybe the frame has rust (if steel) or the cart was driven in saltwater areas and has corrosion. You have to do careful inspection and ask about its history. Used carts often lack any warranty, meaning you'll bear repair costs from day one.
- **Outdated Technology:** An older used cart might lack modern features. For instance, a 10-year-old cart likely has less efficient batteries or less powerful motor than new ones. It may not have LED lights or turn signals if you need them for street use. You

can often retrofit upgrades, but that adds cost. Some older carts also may have limited availability of parts (though major brands have parts available for decades-old models, smaller brands might not).
- **Potential for Higher Maintenance Soon:** You have to consider things like: How old are the tires? Do the brakes need work? Are the shocks or leaf springs worn out? Particularly with batteries – if the seller hasn't replaced them recently, you might be looking at a replacement very soon (a key question to ask: *when were the batteries last replaced?*). Older carts might also need things like new bushings in the suspension or a new drive belt on a gas cart. These aren't deal-breakers, but they are costs you should factor in. A great deal on a used cart can sour if you have to dump a lot of money into repairs immediately.
- **No Warranty:** Unless you buy a "certified pre-owned" cart from a dealer, used sales are typically **as-is** (with no warranty). That means if something goes wrong a week after purchase, it's on you. Some dealers do offer limited warranties on used carts they've refurbished – that can provide some assurance, so it's worth checking if buying from a dealer (we'll cover that in Chapter 6).

Deciding Factors – New vs Used:

Ask yourself a few key questions:

1. **What is my budget?** If you have, say, $3,000 to spend, you're likely looking at used carts (or very bare-bones new ones, but even those might be above that). If you have $10,000+, you could comfortably consider new – though you might still opt used to save money.
2. **How will I use the cart, and how soon do I need it?** If you're relying on this cart for daily transport in a community and you can't afford downtime, a new cart with a warranty might provide more reliability. If it's for occasional fun or secondary use, you might be willing to tinker with a used one.
3. **Am I comfortable evaluating and potentially fixing a used cart?** If you have some mechanical knowledge or are willing to learn basic maintenance, a used cart can be a great DIY project. On the other hand, if you prefer something turn-key, new is the safer bet.
4. **How long do I plan to keep it?** If this is a long-term ownership (5-10 years), new might pay off since you'll use up much of the cart's life. If you might upgrade in a couple of years, a used cart might hold its value better

proportionally (and you won't lose as much in depreciation).

Resale Tip: Golf carts, especially electric ones, often have their steepest depreciation in the first few years then hold value if maintained. This is because once a cart is, say, 4 or 5 years old, its value is largely based on condition (batteries, appearance, etc.) rather than age. A well-maintained 8-year-old cart might sell for not much less than a 4-year-old one if both have new batteries and similar features. This means buying a lightly used cart can be a sweet spot – someone else paid the new premium, and you get a lot of life left.

In summary, **new carts offer peace of mind and the latest features at a higher price**, while **used carts offer value and variety but require due diligence**. There's also a middle ground some people choose: buying a used cart and then doing a refurbishment – for example, new batteries, a new paint job or body panels, fresh tires, etc., effectively making it "like new" in function for less than the cost of a brand new unit.

Now that you have an idea of new vs. used, the next logical consideration is *where to buy your golf cart*. There are dealerships, private sales, online marketplaces, and even custom builders. Chapter 6 will explore these avenues and give tips on navigating each source to find the cart you want.

Chapter 6:
Where to Buy – Dealerships, Private Sellers, and Online Marketplaces

ONCE YOU'VE DECIDED on the type of cart you want (gas or electric, new or used, etc.), the next step is to find the right place to buy it. The buying experience can differ greatly depending on whether you go through a **licensed dealership, a private seller, or an online platform**. Each has its pros and cons, and knowing what to expect will help you navigate the process smoothly.

Buying from a Dealership:

Dealerships (especially those authorized by major brands) are often the first choice for new carts, but many also sell used and refurbished units. Here's what to consider:

- **Expertise and Guidance:** Dealers who specialize in golf carts can be a wealth of knowledge. They can guide you through options, let you test drive different models, and help match you with a cart that fits your needs. This is particularly helpful if you're new to golf carts – you can ask lots of questions and get on-the-spot answers.
- **Inventory and Customization:** A large dealership may have a variety of models in stock – new ones from different brands, plus used trade-ins. They might also have demonstration models. You can often try a few carts on-site. Many dealers also offer customization services: for example, they might offer to lift a cart, add rear seat kits, change body color, or install accessories before you take it home (usually for an added cost, of course).
- **Warranty and Support:** New carts come with manufacturer warranties, which dealers will handle for you (servicing, etc.). Some dealers also give limited warranties on used carts they sell – for instance, they might warranty the batteries for 6 months or offer a 30-day full warranty on a refurbished cart. They likely have a service department, so future maintenance or repairs can be done by

professionals who know the product. This ongoing support is a comfort to many buyers.
- **Financing Options:** Dealers often provide financing plans for new (and sometimes used) carts, just like car dealerships. They may work with financing companies or the manufacturer's financing arm. If you prefer to pay over time, a dealer can set that up – something that's not available if you buy from a private party.
- **Credibility and Regulation:** Unlike private sellers, dealerships often operate under business regulations and licenses. While the golf cart industry isn't as strictly regulated as auto sales, a reputable dealer has a reputation to uphold. They are usually more careful in representing a cart's condition accurately, since their business depends on customer satisfaction. As noted by experts, dealerships present a **more reliable option** because they vet and service the carts they sell, offering buyers more peace of mind.

On the downside, buying from a dealer can be a bit more expensive – you pay for that service and support. However, many buyers feel the premium is worth it. It's also worth mentioning that some areas have **golf cart superstores or large retailers (like motorsports dealers)** that sell carts alongside ATVs or other vehicles. These can be similar to specialized dealers in approach.

Buying from a Private Seller (Classifieds/Person-to-Person):

This includes finding carts via local classifieds, Craigslist, Facebook Marketplace, community bulletin boards, or word-of-mouth. Many used golf carts are sold this way.

- **Potentially Lower Prices:** Private sellers may price their carts more competitively because they're often just looking to make a sale without the overhead of a business. You might find a great deal if someone is moving or simply doesn't need their cart anymore and wants it gone.
- **Room for Negotiation:** In private sales, prices are usually negotiable. With good research on what comparable carts are worth, you can often haggle a bit and land on a fair price. Private sellers might also throw in extras (like a charger, cover, or spare parts) as part of the deal.
- **Caution and Diligence Needed:** The flip side is you *really* have to do your homework. Since private sales aren't regulated, the responsibility is on you to verify everything. Always **inspect the cart thoroughly and**

take it for a test drive. If you're not mechanically savvy, consider bringing along a friend who is, or even hiring a local golf cart mechanic to inspect it (some might do this for a small fee). You should ask a lot of questions: How old is it? How was it used (on a course, in a neighborhood, commercially)? Any modifications done? How often were batteries maintained or when were they last replaced? Has it ever been in an accident or tipped over? The *history* is very important.

- **Higher Risk:** Because there's no warranty, anything that happens post-sale is your issue. Ensure the seller provides any paperwork they have (receipts for new batteries or recent service, manuals, etc.). If the cart is supposed to be street legal and registered, make sure the **title or registration documents** are properly signed over so you can register it yourself. In some states, golf carts (especially LSVs) have titles like cars do.
- **Avoiding Scams:** Use common sense – if a deal sounds too good to be true ("2020 model cart, barely used, for $1,000!"), be wary. Unfortunately, scams exist. Only deal locally and in person. Verify the identity of the seller if possible and that they legitimately own the cart (match the name on any registration or bill of sale). If using an online marketplace,

read reviews or ratings of the person if available.

Online Marketplaces and Auctions:

There are also formal online marketplaces specifically for golf carts (for example, some websites aggregate dealer listings nationwide), as well as general ones like eBay.

- **Wider Search Radius:** Online, you can see carts from all over. This is helpful if local inventory is scarce. You might find exactly what you want in another state. However, you'll have to consider shipping costs if it's far away (which can be several hundred dollars to freight a cart, or a long drive if you pick up).
- **Detailed Listings:** Good online listings will have plenty of photos and details. Study those closely. Ask the seller questions via messaging. Request specific pictures if something isn't clear (like close-up of the battery compartment, or the tires).
- **Buyer Protection:** If using a platform like eBay Motors, there might be some buyer protection or structured process (like using an escrow service, etc.). Still, many of the same caveats as private sales apply – you might not see it in person until after purchase, so there's

a leap of faith. Try to arrange an inspection period or return option, if possible.
- **Auction Deals:** Golf course fleets often get sold at auctions when courses upgrade their carts. If you're adventurous, you could look for local auctions or estate sales. Sometimes you can get fleet carts cheaply, but be careful – fleet carts may have had heavy use (though also regular maintenance). Auction sales are typically as-is and final.

Rental Fleets and Trade-Ins: Another avenue: Some golf courses or rental companies sell their used carts after a few years of service. These carts (especially from courses) may be base models and could be well-maintained on schedule. However, they also might have a lot of hours on them. If you find a course selling off carts, you could snag one at a decent price, but inspect for wear (like steering play, brake wear, and of course battery age if electric). Similarly, some individuals upgrade and trade in their old cart to a dealer – those trade-ins often become the used stock dealers resell (often after refurbishing).

Dealers vs. Private – Who to Trust?: The golf cart industry isn't as heavily regulated as auto sales, so whether you go dealer or private, a lot comes down to the specific people you're dealing with. A **reputable dealer** with good reviews and long-standing community presence is generally a safe bet. But a *knowledgeable private seller* who took good care of their cart can also provide a great buying experience and outcome. Conversely, there are occasional stories of less scrupulous dealers overcharging or misrepresenting, and likewise unscrupulous individuals. So, do your due diligence either way. One advantage with dealers is you often have some recourse (e.g., you can call and complain or leave reviews if something was misrepresented), whereas with a private sale, once it's done, it's done.

Documentation: Regardless of source, always get a **bill of sale** that includes the cart's serial number, the sale date, price, and the names/signatures of buyer and seller. If the cart is street legal or titled, make sure you get the proper title document or transferable registration. This will save headaches at the DMV if you need to register it. If it's just an off-road cart, you at least want proof of purchase for your records.

To wrap up: *Buying from a dealer* offers convenience, support, and assurance, ideal for those who want a smoother, lower-risk experience (with a likely higher price). *Buying privately or online* can save money and yield a perfectly good cart, but it puts more responsibility on you to ensure you're getting what you expect.

Next, we'll discuss the key features and specifications you should evaluate on any cart you consider – essentially a buyer's checklist of what to look for, which will be useful no matter where you end up shopping.

Chapter 7:
Key Features and Specifications to Evaluate

WHEN COMPARING GOLF CARTS, especially if you're looking at multiple options, it's important to understand the key features and specifications that differentiate one cart from another. This chapter serves as a guide to the *critical factors you should evaluate* before buying. Think of it as a checklist of questions: Does the cart meet my needs in this aspect? How does Cart A compare to Cart B on this spec?

1. Seating Capacity: Golf carts come in various seating configurations – the most common being 2-seater, 4-seater, and 6-seater. A standard 2-seater is great for solo riders or couples (and of course, golf bags). If you have family or plan to shuttle friends, a 4-seater (which often is a 2-seater with a rear-facing bench added) is convenient. Six-seaters are longer and have three rows (two forward-facing benches and one rear-facing, or sometimes all forward-facing in a stretched limo style). More seats mean a higher cost – *on average a four-passenger golf cart ranges from $10,000 to $15,000 new, and six-passenger models from $12,000 to $16,000+*. If you only occasionally need extra seats, you can consider a 2-seater and use a rear seat kit (many can be installed to convert the back into a seat). But if it's frequent, buying one built for 4 or 6 is better for stability and space.

2. Motor/Engine Power: For electric carts, check the motor's power (measured in horsepower or kilowatts) and type. Some newer electric carts have **AC motors** instead of traditional DC motors – AC motors are generally more efficient, have more torque and speed, and often appear in higher-end models (like Yamaha Drive2 AC, etc.). The controller amperage also matters (bigger controllers can deliver more current for torque). For gas carts, engine displacement (in cc) and HP are the figures – e.g., a 11.5 HP 357cc Yamaha, or a 14 HP 429cc Club Car engine. While you might not find all these specs easily, if performance is key (like pulling power or hill climbing), try to get a sense of the cart's rating. User reviews or the test drive might reveal more than the numbers – some 8 HP carts perform as well as other 11 HP ones due to gearing.

3. Speed: Most standard golf carts are limited to around 15 mph by the factory (for golf course safety). However, many models can go faster with slight tweaks. "Street legal" LSV carts are usually set to 20-25 mph. If buying new, the dealer can often configure the speed for you (within legal limits). If buying used, you might find some have speed modifications. Be cautious: going too fast (beyond 25 mph) can be dangerous in a golf cart chassis not meant for it (risk of tipping or crashing). That said, if you need a cart that can do near 25 mph for street use, verify that the cart can achieve that. Some older carts might max at ~13-14 mph unless modified.

4. Range/Battery Capacity (Electric): As discussed in Chapter 4, if it's electric, know the voltage (36V vs 48V etc.) and ideally the amp-hour rating of the batteries. Ask the seller or dealer how far it typically goes on a charge. If you'll use it around a community, consider how many miles your typical day's usage will be. Remember things like carrying a lot of passengers or going up hills will reduce range. If you're concerned, maybe look for a lithium battery model or higher capacity lead-acid pack. If it's gas, range is usually not an issue as long as you can refill, but check fuel tank size (usually 5-6 gallons, which might last several days or weeks of typical use).

5. Charging System (Electric): What kind of charger comes with it? Modern carts have automatic smart chargers – ideally 48V ones that shut off when complete. Some may even have onboard chargers (built into the cart). Confirm that the charger works and is compatible with your electrical supply. If it's a used cart, a new charger can be a few hundred dollars, so getting a good one included is important.

6. Frame and Body Material: As mentioned, **Club Car** and some others use aluminum frames, which are rust-proof – a plus if you live in a humid or coastal area. Steel frames (found in E-Z-GO, Yamaha, and many others) are strong but can rust if the paint/coating fails and moisture gets to them. Check underneath the cart or under the battery compartment for any corrosion. Also, note the body panels: are they plastic (which won't rust but can crack) or metal? Most are plastic/fiberglass which is fine; just check for cracks or repaired sections on used carts.

7. Tires and Suspension: Look at the tires' condition and type. Are they turf tires (smooth-ish tread) or all-terrain? If you plan to drive on pavement a lot, a street tread may give a quieter ride. Off-road or knobby tires are great for trails but can wear faster on pavement and make more noise. Check suspension: do a bounce test on each corner (push down and see if it rebounds smoothly). Listen for squeaks or clunks on the test drive – that could indicate worn shocks or bushings. If the cart is lifted (has a lift kit for higher ground clearance and big tires), ensure it was done properly – the steering should not feel too loose and the cart should track straight. Lifted carts can be a bit tippier on turns, so take a slow turn during test drive to feel stability.

8. Brakes: Most carts have only rear brakes. Make sure they stop the cart effectively and evenly. If it pulls to one side, a brake might be adjusted poorly or contaminated. Some newer or upgraded carts have four-wheel brakes or disc brake conversions – those are nice features for better stopping power, especially on faster carts. Also check the parking brake – does it hold well on a slope?

9. Lights and Street-Legal Features: If you need a street-legal cart/LSV, you'll want headlights, taillights, turn signals, brake lights, reflectors, horn, windshield, and mirrors at a minimum. Many carts can be fitted with a "street legal kit." When evaluating, see if these are already installed if that's important for you. If not, factor in the cost to add them. Also, a **17-digit VIN** is required for a truly street-legal LSV (usually assigned by the manufacturer for LSV models). If the cart is an LSV, check for the VIN plate. If not, and you want to register it, you might have to go through a state inspection process to get one assigned.

10. Accessories and Extras: Consider what comes with the cart:

- **Windshield:** Fold-down windshields are common and help in rain or chilly mornings.
- **Roof/Canopy:** Most have a roof over the front seats, some extended to cover rear seats. If you want one, check it's there; they can be added but are a few hundred dollars.
- **Enclosure/Curtains:** For all-weather use, some carts include zippered vinyl enclosures. Nice for rain or cold – see if one is included.
- **Mirrors:** Side mirrors and/or a panoramic rear-view mirror are inexpensive but useful additions.
- **Seating Upgrades:** Are the seats stock or upgraded? High-back or cushioned seats can be more comfortable and look nice.
- **Storage:** Some carts have locking glove boxes, under-seat storage trays, or cooler/storage boxes under the rear seat. Not critical, but note what's included.
- **Stereo/Tech:** It's not uncommon for custom carts to have a radio or Bluetooth sound system, or even a built-in GPS for golf. If you care about tunes on the go, check for this.
- **Tow Hitch:** If you plan to tow a small trailer or pull a yard cart, see if there's a hitch receiver or if one can be added.

- **Charger & Charging Port:** As mentioned, ensure the charger is included. Also check the charging port on the cart isn't loose or damaged.
- **Other:** Some sellers throw in a weatherproof cover, spare tire, or other goodies. It's worth asking what's included.

11. Aesthetics and Custom Work: Look at the overall cosmetic condition. Faded paint or body panels can be repainted or replaced fairly easily, but it's a negotiating point. If a cart has a custom paint job or wraps, make sure you like it (or be prepared to refinish). Custom lighting (underglow lights, etc.) or other modifications might hint at an enthusiast owner – possibly good (if they took care of it) or possibly meaning it was driven hard. Try to gauge how well any custom wiring or mods were done (neat and professional, or messy tape and twist jobs).

12. Serial Number and Year: It's helpful to verify the year of the cart via its serial number with the manufacturer if possible. Sellers should know the year, but sometimes carts are rebuilt or mislabeled. Knowing the exact model year lets you look up specs and ensure parts availability. As one pro tip: **verify the manufacture year through the serial number** – different brands encode the year in different ways (for example, some Club Car serials start with the year, E-Z-GO might have the date code on a plate, etc.). You can call a dealer or check online databases for that brand.

By carefully evaluating these features and specs, you'll avoid surprises and make sure the cart you choose aligns with how you intend to use it. It can be useful to make a checklist (we'll provide one in Chapter 13) and check off these items when inspecting a cart.

Now that we know *what to look for* in a cart, let's explore the major **brands and models** on the market. Knowing the players (Club Car vs E-Z-GO vs Yamaha, etc.) and their notable models will give you context as you shop, which is up next in Chapter 8.

Chapter 8:
Major Golf Cart Brands and Models – A Buyer's Overview

Just like cars, golf carts have a few big-name manufacturers and a range of models. Each brand has its strengths and unique features, and knowing a bit about them can guide your decision or at least help you understand what you're looking at. In this chapter, we'll give a brief overview of the **major golf cart brands** and some popular models from each, along with any distinguishing characteristics.

1. Club Car:

Overview: Club Car is one of the top golf cart brands and has been in the game since 1958. The company started in Texas and later moved to Augusta, Georgia (famous for Augusta National Golf Club). Club Car became a major competitor especially after being acquired by Bill Stevens in the 1960s and later seeing significant growth from the late 1970s onward. They are now a division of Ingersoll Rand, a large industrial company.

What They're Known For: Club Car carts are renowned for their **aluminum frame**, which means they won't rust – a big advantage in humid or coastal areas. They're also known for good build quality and durability. Club Car was a pioneer in introducing **innovative models** – for example, the Club Car DS in 1980, which was a stylish design that became ubiquitous on courses, and the **Carryall** utility series for non-golf uses. They have a reputation for being premium carts.

Popular Models:
- *Club Car Precedent:* This model (introduced mid-2000s) became a standard in fleets and personal use. It has a sleek design and came in electric or gas. In recent years, Club Car has evolved the Precedent into newer lines.
- *Club Car Onward:* The Onward is Club Car's modern consumer lineup – available in 2, 4, and 6 passenger versions, with options for lifted suspension, different power options (including lithium batteries), and lots of custom colors and accessories. Essentially, it's a factory customizable cart aimed at personal owners.

- *Club Car Villager & Carryall:* These names cover their utility and people-mover carts. The Villager can be a transport vehicle (often 6 or 8 seat shuttles seen at resorts or campuses), while Carryall typically refers to flat-bed or cargo utility carts.
- *Club Car Tempo:* A model often sold to golf courses in recent years, which is similar to the Precedent but aimed at fleet use with some tech improvements.

2. E-Z-GO:

Overview: E-Z-GO is another heavyweight, founded in 1954 in Georgia. They became part of Textron Inc. (a large conglomerate) and have produced huge numbers of carts for both golf course fleets and consumer use.

Known For: E-Z-GO carts traditionally have steel frames (so watch for rust), and they popularized some electric technologies. They introduced the **TXT** model and later the **RXV** which boasted an advanced AC drive system and regenerative braking. E-Z-GO also has the **Cushman** brand under its umbrella (Cushman, founded in 1955, became part of Textron, and those are usually heavier-duty industrial carts). E-Z-GO has a wide dealer network and parts are generally easy to find.

Popular Models:
- *E-Z-GO TXT:* A classic model that's been around for a long time (with updates). Many older (1990s-2000s) E-Z-GOs you find used will be TXT variants. Available in gas or electric. Reliable and simple, a workhorse of golf fleets.
- *E-Z-GO RXV:* Introduced around 2008, the RXV is known for its **AC electric motor** and a technology that makes it so the parking brake engages automatically when the vehicle stops (electromagnetic brake). The AC system gives it strong torque and efficiency. RXVs are common on courses and also as upgraded personal carts.
- *E-Z-GO Freedom/Valor/Express:* E-Z-GO markets consumer versions often under names like Freedom (basically a TXT or RXV with street-legal package), Valor (a budget-friendly basic cart), and Express (their line of lifted or multi-passenger carts for off-road or neighborhood use). The Express S4 or L6 are 4 or 6 seat lifted carts appealing to those wanting a ready-made lifted buggy.

3. Yamaha:

Overview: Yamaha, the same company known for motorcycles and musical instruments, also has a golf car division. They entered the golf cart market in 1977 and have been a strong competitor since.

Known For: Yamaha carts are praised for their **smooth ride and strong gas engines**. In fact, Yamaha's gas carts often use their own small engines and are reputed to be some of the quietest gas carts (especially their newer Quietech EFI models which have sound-dampening – they advertise them as the quietest gas carts on the market). They've also been innovative: Yamaha introduced the first electronic fuel injection (EFI) gas cart (the Drive2 EFI) and AC electric models in recent years.

Popular Models:
- *Yamaha G-Series:* Older Yamaha models (G1 through G22) from the 80s, 90s, early 2000s are often still around. The G29 was also known as "Yamaha Drive". If you see references like G16, G29, etc., that's the model numbering scheme.
- *Yamaha Drive / Drive2:* The Drive (also called G29) came out around 2007, and was a big step in design for Yamaha, with a modular frame and better suspension. The Drive2 is the updated version introduced

around 2017. The Drive2 is available in gas (Quietech EFI) or electric (with AC motors). These are commonly sold both for golf courses and personal use. They have modern styling and features like USB ports, automotive-style dash, etc.
- *Yamaha Adventurer / UMAX:* Yamaha's line for utility or lifted carts. The Adventurer Sport is like a lifted 2+2 (4-seater) version of the Drive. The UMAX models are more utility oriented (with cargo beds, etc.) for work use.

4. Other Notable Players:
- **Columbia ParCar:** Columbia (which acquired the Harley Davidson golf cart line in the early 1980s) has produced various industrial and personal carts. Not as common for personal golf carts these days, but you might encounter them.
- **Cushman:** Now essentially E-Z-GO's sister brand for utility vehicles (often heavier duty, industrial carts, or personnel carriers). If you want a small utility truck-like cart, Cushman Hauler or Shuttle might be in that category.
- **Star EV, Icon, Advanced EV, etc.:** In the past decade, a number of companies (some based in China, with US distribution) have

entered the market with street-legal LSVs and carts that often come fully loaded for less cost than the big brands. Star EV, ICON, Advanced EV, Epic, Evolution – these are some names that you might see. They often use standardized parts (like common 48V electric systems) and boast features like lithium batteries or fancy lighting at lower price points. While they are gaining popularity, one consideration is parts and service – since they are newer, ensure there's a dealer or support for them near you. These carts can be a good value if you want a new cart with many features but at a lower cost than, say, a Club Car Onward.

- **Polaris GEM and Others:** If your focus is more on a truly street-legal low-speed vehicle, the GEM (by Polaris) is a small NEV that's more car-like (doors, etc.). There are also specialty brands like Garia (luxury golf carts made in Denmark with high-end finishes) – pricey but very stylish. Those are less common, but if you're looking at the high end, they're out there.

Brand Differences: Often the choice of brand comes down to what you have experience with or what dealers are nearby. All three major brands (Club Car,

E-Z-GO, Yamaha) produce quality carts. Each has slightly different feel:

- Club Cars might have a slight edge in refinement and corrosion resistance (aluminum frame).
- E-Z-GOs have very customizable platforms and a huge after-market community (especially for modifying TXT/RXV).
- Yamahas have arguably the best gasoline technology (their EFI gas carts are very fuel-efficient and quiet) and a very solid build as well.

It's a bit like comparing Ford, Chevy, Toyota in cars – loyalists exist for each, but objectively they all get the job done. If you are buying used, condition and care matter more than brand. A well-maintained 10-year-old Yamaha is better than a beat-up 5-year-old Club Car, for example.

Production Years and Generations: It might help to know roughly the eras:

- Pre-2000: Club Car DS (electric/gas), E-Z-GO Marathon then Medalist models, Yamaha G-series (G1-G16 etc.). Those you see as older, cheaper carts often.
- 2000s: Club Car Precedent (came mid-2000s), E-Z-GO TXT (early 2000s), Yamaha G22/Drive (late 2000s).

- 2010s: E-Z-GO RXV (2008+), Yamaha Drive2 (2017+), Club Car onward (2017+), with lithium options starting to appear towards late 2010s.
- 2020s: Wider adoption of lithium, more tech (like Bluetooth speakers integrated, better lighting, etc.), and more entrants (Icon, etc., as mentioned).

Knowing the brand and model will also help when you look up accessories or parts. Many third-party manufacturers specify compatibility by model (e.g., "fits Club Car Precedent 2004-2019", "for E-Z-GO TXT 1996-2013", etc.). So once you have a cart, it's good to know exactly what it is.

Finally, brand can impact **resale value**. The big three (Club Car, E-Z-GO, Yamaha) generally hold value well because people recognize them and trust them. The newer brands might depreciate more until they establish a track record, but that could also mean a bargain on the used market.

Now that we have covered brands, the next chapter shifts gears to something fun: customizing your golf cart! Many buyers love to personalize their carts with accessories, custom paint, lift kits, and more. We'll go through common customization options and what to know about them in Chapter 9.

Chapter 9:
Customization and Accessories – Making the Cart Your Own

One of the joys of owning a golf cart is the ability to customize it. Just like car enthusiasts add mods to their vehicles, golf cart owners often personalize their carts for both aesthetic and functional reasons. Whether you want a flashy head-turner or a practical utility machine, there are countless **accessories and upgrades** available. In this chapter, we explore popular customization options, their benefits, and some considerations before you start modifying.

Lift Kits and Off-Road Upgrades:

Lifting a golf cart (installing a lift kit) is a common modification, especially for those who want to use the cart on rougher terrain or just like the lifted look (similar to a lifted pickup truck). A lift kit raises the cart's ride height by a few inches (commonly 3", 4",

6" lifts) and allows for larger, more rugged tires. **Pros:** A lifted cart with big all-terrain tires can traverse trails, mud, or uneven ground much better than a stock cart with small tires. It also gives a higher seating position and can look really cool, resembling an ATV. **Cons:** The center of gravity is higher, which can increase risk of tipping on sharp turns – always drive a lifted cart a bit more carefully, especially on pavement. Also, lifting may add some strain on the suspension and steering if not done right. If you buy a cart that's already lifted, inspect the install quality: everything should be tight, with proper components (for example, drop axle lift vs spindle lift – each has different pros/cons). Lift kits range from a few hundred dollars for basic spindle lifts to $1000+ for high-end long-travel suspension lifts. Remember that **bigger tires affect gearing** – they will make the cart go faster but with slightly less torque, unless you also upgrade the gears or motor. Many lifted carts also get upgraded controllers or motors to compensate and get better torque for those big tires.

Wheels and Tires:

Even without a lift, swapping wheels and tires can change your cart's look and feel. Chrome or alloy wheels in various styles are available, often in 10", 12", or 14" diameters (stock cart wheels are usually

8" steel rims with caps). Low-profile street tires on big rims can give a cart a sporty look (commonly seen on customized neighborhood carts), whereas knobby off-road tires give a rugged look. Make sure any tire upgrade maintains proper clearance. Also, consider ride quality: larger wheels with low-profile tires may ride a bit stiffer (less sidewall to absorb bumps), whereas smaller wheels with balloon tires ride softer.

Paint, Body, and Aesthetics:

Custom paint jobs or vinyl wraps are popular for making a cart stand out. You might have seen carts painted in sports team colors, camouflage for hunting, or candy-apple metallic flake for that hot-rod vibe. If you're artistically inclined, the cart's body panels are a great canvas. There are also aftermarket bodies that can dramatically change the look – for example, kits that make a cart look like a small Jeep, a '57 Chevy, or other novelty designs. These can be expensive but very unique. If painting, use an automotive-grade process for durability, or wraps for easily reversible designs. Don't forget details like seat upholstery – custom two-tone seats or embroidery can add a nice touch.

Lighting and Electrical Accessories:

Lighting upgrades serve both style and function. Common additions:

- **LED Light Bars** for off-roading or better night visibility (often mounted on the roof or front brush guard).
- **Underbody glow lights** or wheel well lights for flair during night rides.
- **Upgraded Headlights/Taillights:** If your cart didn't have lights, adding a street-legal light kit is often the first step. Many kits offer LED headlights which are bright and low draw.
- **Turn signals and Horn:** needed for street use, but also convenient in community settings for safety.
- **12V Outlets or USB Ports:** Many newer carts have them standard; they're easy to add to charge phones or plug in accessories.
- **Sound Systems:** It's quite popular to install a stereo in a golf cart. This could be as simple as a Bluetooth speaker mounted somewhere, or a full-on car stereo unit with marine speakers mounted under the dash or in the roof. There are purpose-built overhead radio consoles for carts that fit in the roof. Just ensure the cart's electrical system (and

converter, if electric) can handle the extra load.

- **Fans or Heaters:** If you use the cart in very hot or cold climates, you can add 12V fans or even small heaters (often propane or 12V electric) to an enclosed cart. For example, some carts have a little ceramic heater for those chilly morning drives (works best if you have a rain enclosure to keep heat in).

Functional Add-ons:

Think about how you'll use the cart day-to-day and consider these:

- **Rear Seat Kits / Flip Seats:** If your cart is a two-seater but you want to occasionally carry more people, a rear flip seat kit is a great addition. It replaces the bagwell with a bench seat. Many flip seats have a platform that flips over to become a flatbed for cargo – very handy for hauling groceries, yard tools, or coolers. Make sure the kit is sturdy and has a safety bar or backrest for the rear passengers. Also, if you carry 4 people often, consider upgrading rear springs to heavy-duty ones to support the weight.
- **Cargo Beds:** For utility use, you might prefer a proper cargo bed instead of seats. Some beds are aluminum dump beds (manual or

electric dump) – great for landscaping or farm use.
- **Roof Racks / Storage:** You can add overhead storage baskets (like a shelf below the roof at the front for light items), or roof racks on top of the canopy for carrying fishing rods, ladders, etc.
- **Windshield:** If your cart doesn't have one, this is a must in our opinion – getting wind in your face at 20 mph on a chilly day isn't fun. A flip-down windshield is versatile (up in cold/rain, down for breeze on nice days). Some even come with wipers (manual or electric wipers are required for street use in some jurisdictions).
- **Mirrors:** A wide-angle rear mirror and side mirrors greatly improve safety. In tight communities or busy paths, it's good to see behind you.
- **Seat Belts:** If you have a street-legal cart or carry kids, installing seat belts is wise. Kits are available that bolt into the cart frame under the seat.
- **Lift Wind Guard:** Minor accessory – some people add a little skirt or guard at the bottom of the cart (especially lifted ones) to reduce how much dust and debris swirl up from underneath.

Performance Upgrades:

For those who want more speed or torque:

- **High-Speed Gears:** In the differential of electric carts, swapping to a set of high-speed gears can increase top speed (at the expense of some torque).
- **Motor/Controller Upgrades:** A common route – replacing the electric motor with a higher torque or higher speed motor, and upgrading the controller to supply more amperage. This can make an electric cart a real performer (just be sure the rest of the cart – brakes, etc., can handle it).
- **High Torque Clutches (Gas carts):** For gas carts, one can change the clutch sheaves or springs to get more low-end torque for hill climbing or adjust speed.
- **Engine Swaps:** Some enthusiasts even put larger engines (like a 18hp Vanguard V-twin or similar) in gas carts for major power increase. This is an advanced mod and beyond the scope of what a typical buyer would do, but it's out there in the modding community.
- **Lithium Battery Upgrade:** As discussed before, swapping lead-acid batteries for a lithium pack can improve speed (due to lighter weight) and give a more consistent

power output through the discharge cycle, often yielding a bit more performance.

A Note on Customization and Value: It's worth noting that customizing a cart is primarily for *your enjoyment*. It may not dramatically increase resale value – sometimes it might, but often you won't recoup all the money spent on mods. So, do it because you want those features, not purely as an investment. Exception: a cleanly done customization, like a beautiful paint job and new seats, can make a cart far more appealing to buyers and could set it apart to sell faster or for a bit more. But a heavily personalized theme (say, painted with your favorite sports team) might actually need the "right buyer" later on.

Budget and Plan Your Upgrades: If you're buying new, you might opt to roll in some accessories at purchase (like if a dealer offers to add a lift kit or rear seat). If buying used, you might find a cart that already has some of these upgrades, which can save money. Make a list of must-haves vs nice-to-haves. Safety items (lights, belts, mirrors) should be higher priority if not already present. Performance upgrades should be done judiciously – ensure you don't exceed what's safe for your cart's design.

Finally, always source quality parts from reputable vendors, especially for critical components like lift kits or electrical parts. Poor-quality accessories can fail or even be dangerous (e.g., flimsy seat brackets or cheap wiring that could cause fires). There's a big aftermarket for golf carts, and many community forums where you can get advice on what brands to trust.

After customizing, your cart truly becomes *your own*. But whether stock or modified, if you want to drive it beyond just the golf course, you need to think about the rules of the road. Next, in Chapter 10, we'll cover the important **street legal and regulatory considerations** to ensure you're riding within the law and safely.

Chapter 10:
Street Legal and Regulatory Considerations

GOLF CARTS OPERATE in a gray area between recreational vehicles and road vehicles. Depending on where you live and how you want to use your cart, there are laws and regulations to consider. In this chapter, we'll clarify what it means to have a **street legal golf cart (often called a Low-Speed Vehicle or LSV)**, and other rules such as where you can drive, who can drive, and whether you need insurance or registration.

What Makes a Golf Cart "Street Legal"?

To legally drive a golf cart on public roads (beyond just crossing at golf course intersections), the cart usually needs to meet the definition of a **Low-Speed Vehicle (LSV)** under federal and state law. In the U.S., federal regulations (via NHTSA) define an

LSV as a four-wheeled vehicle with a top speed of 20-25 mph. LSVs are required to have certain safety equipment. Here are the **federal requirements for street-legal LSVs** (which essentially turn a golf cart into an LSV):

- **Lights:** Headlights, tail lights, and brake lights, plus turn signals front and rear. Basically, it needs to be as visible as a car in the dark.
- **Mirrors:** Both exterior (side) mirrors and an interior rear-view mirror.
- **Windshield:** A front windshield made of automotive safety glass. Some jurisdictions also require a windshield wiper (even if manual hand-operated).
- **Seat Belts:** Seat belts for each seating position (implied in federal LSV rules under occupant safety).
- **Horn:** An audible horn, just like a car.
- **Reflectors:** Reflex reflectors on the sides and corners (these are the little red/orange reflectors you see on cars).
- **Speed Capability:** It must be able to go at least 20 mph but not more than 25 mph by design.
- **Vehicle Identification Number (VIN):** The vehicle should have a 17-digit VIN assigned.

- **Parking Brake:** A functional parking brake (most carts have this anyway).
- **Weight Limit:** By definition, LSVs are often limited to a certain weight (around 3,000 lbs gross weight, which all golf carts fall under easily).

If a golf cart has all the above, it can be classified and registered as a low-speed vehicle. Many manufacturers produce **LSV versions** of their carts (often sold as "street legal golf carts") that come with this equipment and a VIN. If you are converting a regular cart, you can buy street-legal kits to add the necessary bits, but getting a VIN and registration might require inspection by the DMV.

Where Can You Drive an LSV?

Even if street-legal, LSVs are typically restricted to roads with speed limits of 35 mph or less. This means you can't take it on highways or major thoroughfares. They're meant for neighborhoods, downtown areas, or rural roads where speeds are low. Many communities (like retirement villages, beach towns, etc.) specifically allow and accommodate golf cart LSVs on their roads. Always check local city ordinances – some cities allow golf carts on certain streets, sometimes even if not full LSVs, with specific rules (like daylight only, or requiring a slow-moving vehicle emblem).

Driver's License and Age Requirements:

In virtually all places, to drive a golf cart on public streets, the driver must have a valid driver's license, just as they would for a car. The typical minimum age is 16 with a license. On private property (like a golf course or private community), rules may be more lenient, but it's generally unsafe and illegal in many states for children to operate a motorized cart on public roads. Some states have specific minimum ages (for example, some states say 14 on certain designated roads in communities, but that's not common). It's crucial to enforce this – golf carts can be dangerous in inexperienced hands, and accidents have happened with underage drivers.

Insurance:

Do you need insurance for a golf cart? If you're driving on public roads, **yes, you likely do or should carry insurance**. Many states require at least liability insurance for an LSV, similar to a car (Arizona, for instance, requires it for any on-road use). Even if not mandated, consider that a golf cart can cause injury or damage in an accident, and you want to be protected. Golf cart insurance can cover liability, collision, theft, etc., much like auto insurance. It's generally quite affordable – often much less than auto insurance. If you only use the cart on private property or golf courses, insurance might not be legally required, but check if your homeowner's policy covers any incidents (sometimes it might cover liability on your property). If you financed the cart, the lender might require comprehensive/collision coverage, just like a car loan would. Major insurers like Progressive, Geico, etc., offer golf cart insurance policies or add-ons. According to experts, insurance requirements vary by state, but **liability coverage is often required when using a cart on public roads**, and even when not required, it's wise to have coverage.

Registration and Tags:

If your cart is an LSV with a VIN, you will register it through your DMV and get a license plate (and likely a title, just as for a car). This process typically involves showing proof of ownership (bill of sale or MSO from manufacturer), proof of insurance, and possibly passing an inspection. They will issue a plate and registration just like for a car, although sometimes with distinctions (like a special LSV plate). Once registered, you'll have to renew registration periodically (yearly or biennially) and keep insurance active. Some locales might have golf cart permits instead of full registration – for example, certain towns require a yearly fee and inspection decal but not a state DMV plate. Be sure to research your local laws – a quick call to the local DMV or city hall can clarify what's needed.

Off-Road and Private Use:
If you're not planning to drive on public streets, many of the above legal requirements don't apply. You don't need a VIN, you won't get a license plate, and typically you won't be required to have insurance by law (again, maybe consider liability coverage via homeowner's policy or separate policy for peace of mind). However, *private communities and golf courses have their own rules*. For instance, a golf course might require that your cart have certain features or that you sign a liability waiver. A gated community might require you register the cart with the community association and show proof of insurance to use it on their private roads. Check with the relevant authority (HOA, golf club, etc.).

State and Local Variances:
Every state (and often each city) can have slightly different rules on golf carts. Some states have passed laws allowing local jurisdictions to enable golf cart use on certain roads. For example, in Florida, state law allows counties and cities to designate roads for golf cart use (with or without requiring LSV status) and sets a minimum age of 14 for golf cart operation on those designated roads (Florida Statutes

§316.212). In contrast, California treats any street use as requiring LSV compliance and driver's license. Always look up "YourState golf cart laws" to get specifics.

Safety Tips for Street Use:

Even if your cart is fully legal to hit the roads, remember:

- **You are smaller and slower** than a car. Avoid busy roads. Use cart paths or bike lanes if legally allowed. Don't try to mix with fast traffic.
- **Be visible:** Keep lights on, consider adding a reflective slow-moving vehicle triangle if you're going to be on streets where cars might come up behind you quickly. Bright colors or flags can help.
- **Drive defensively:** Assume other drivers may not see you, and certainly may not predict that a golf cart will be on the road. Cross major streets at traffic lights or crosswalks when possible.
- **Follow all traffic laws:** Stop at stop signs, signal your turns, don't drink and drive (yes, DUI laws apply to golf carts as well).
- **Limit night driving:** If you must drive at night, double-check all lights, and maybe

stick to well-lit areas. Depth perception and visibility are tougher in a cart.

Other Regulations:

Some other things to be aware of:

- Noise ordinances (for gas carts) – if you have a loud modified muffler or are driving late, you could be subject to local noise rules.
- Environmental rules – some places (like certain islands or resorts) only allow electric carts due to environmental goals.
- Passenger limits – by law, you shouldn't have more passengers than seats. That means no lap-sitting kids in the eyes of traffic law (safety aside, you could get ticketed for unsecured passenger).
- Where not to drive – sidewalks are usually off-limits unless specifically allowed for carts. Public trails or parks might or might not allow carts – check signage.

In summary, **to enjoy your golf cart to the fullest, make sure you understand the legal requirements for where you plan to drive it**. Converting a cart to street legal can greatly expand its utility (you can run to the store or visit neighbors legally), but it comes with the need for registration, insurance, and prudent driving. If that's not in your interest, you can keep the cart on private property and avoid some red tape, but never take it on public roads.

Next up, Chapter 11 will delve into the ongoing responsibilities of cart ownership: **maintenance and upkeep**. Just like any vehicle, a golf cart needs care to stay in top shape. We'll cover maintenance routines for both electric and gas carts, as well as common repairs and how to maximize your cart's lifespan.

Chapter 11: Maintenance and Upkeep – Keeping Your Cart Running Smoothly

TAKING CARE OF your golf cart is crucial for safety, performance, and longevity. A well-maintained cart can last for decades, while neglect can lead to breakdowns or costly repairs. The good news is that golf cart maintenance is generally simpler and less time-consuming than car maintenance. In this chapter, we outline the key maintenance tasks and schedules for both electric and gas golf carts, and we touch on troubleshooting common issues.

Regular Cleaning and Care:
No matter the type, keep your cart clean. Mud, sand, or chemicals (like fertilizer or salt) can promote corrosion or wear. Rinse off the undercarriage if

you've been driving in areas like beach sand or roads that might have salt. For electric carts, cleaning the battery compartment is important: batteries can vent acid, which causes corrosion. **Check and clean battery terminals** regularly, removing any corrosion (a paste of baking soda and water can neutralize acid on terminals; disconnect the battery pack before cleaning to avoid shorts). Also, keep the top of batteries clean and dry – dirt can cause a tiny bit of current drain between terminals.

The body and seats can be washed with mild soap and water. If the cart has a vinyl enclosure or seat covers, use appropriate cleaners to avoid cracking. For windshields (often acrylic or polycarbonate), avoid harsh chemicals like Windex – use water or a plastic cleaner to prevent fogging or microcracks.

Battery Maintenance (Electric Carts):

We discussed battery care in Chapter 4, but to reiterate key maintenance:

- **Watering:** If you have traditional lead-acid batteries, check water levels in each cell monthly (or more often in hot climates or with heavy use). Use only distilled water and fill to the proper level (just covering the plates, or to the indicator if present). Never

let the plates be exposed to air, as that will cause permanent sulfation and capacity loss.
- **Charging Habits:** After each use (daily), plug the cart in and charge fully. Leaving batteries discharged even for a few days can be detrimental. Most smart chargers will prevent overcharge, so it's okay to leave it plugged in overnight or for the weekend. If storing the cart for long periods (month or more), ensure the batteries are fully charged and then either disconnect them or periodically top-off charge (some chargers have a storage mode that will kick on automatically as needed).
- **Inspection:** Every so often, inspect battery cables for fraying or damage and replace as needed. Also ensure the hold-downs or brackets are secure so batteries aren't sliding around.
- **Battery Life:** As batteries age, their performance drops. If you notice the cart not running as long or slowing down significantly on hills, it might be time to test the batteries. Many auto parts or battery shops can load test deep-cycle batteries. Replacing a whole pack is often recommended so they age uniformly. Battery replacement is one of the biggest maintenance expenses for electric carts

(about $800-$2,000 as noted earlier depending on type), so take care of them to maximize lifespan (3-5 years is average for lead-acid in heavy use, up to 6-8 with meticulous care; lithium batteries can go 10+ years with minimal maintenance).

Gas Cart Engine Maintenance:

Gasoline carts have small engines that require similar maintenance to other small engines:

- **Oil Changes:** Typically every 100-125 hours of operation or at least annually, change the engine oil. Most golf cart engines take just a liter or so of 10W-30 or 10W-40 oil (check manual for grade). There's usually a drain plug under the engine and a fill cap/dipstick on top. Some engines have an oil filter (like Kawasaki engines in some Club Cars), which should be replaced if present; others just have a screen.
- **Air Filter:** Check the air filter element and air box. Clean out any dust or debris. Replace the air filter maybe once a year (or more often in dusty environments). A clogged air filter can hurt performance.
- **Fuel System:** Use fresh gasoline; if storing for winter, add a fuel stabilizer and run the engine a bit to get it through the carb. Some

carts have fuel filters in line – change those if they look dirty (cheap part). Also, periodically inspect fuel lines for cracks.
- **Spark Plug:** Check the spark plug annually. It should be a tan-ish color at the tip. If it's all black and sooty, the engine might be running too rich or burning oil. Replace the plug if it's fouled or at least every couple years regardless (they're inexpensive). Gap the new plug according to spec (commonly around 0.028-0.030 inches, but see manual).
- **Belts:** Gas carts (and even some electric) use a drive belt (and a starter/generator belt). The drive belt is on a CVT pulley system in most carts. Over time, belts can wear and slip. If you notice the cart shuddering on takeoff or a loss of hill-climb power, check the belt – if it sits deep in the pulley or has glazed sides, it may need replacing. Belts might last many years, but it's good to inspect for cracks or fraying yearly.
- **Clutches:** The primary and secondary clutches (the pulleys on the engine and axle) can wear. They have ramp shoes and sliders that might need service. Usually not much maintenance except maybe a bit of lubrication on certain points if specified by the manufacturer. If you hear clunking or

have very jerky starts, a clutch might need repair or replacement.
- **Engine Cooling:** These engines are usually air-cooled. Ensure the cooling fins on the engine are not clogged with dirt or leaves, especially if the cart has been run through debris. Also make sure any shrouds or cooling fans are intact. Engine overheating is rare if everything is stock and clean.
- **Winterizing:** If you don't use the gas cart in winter, either run the carb dry (shut fuel and run till it stalls) or add stabilizer. It's also a good idea to disconnect the battery or keep a trickle charger on the starter battery to keep it from draining over winter.

Tires and Brakes:
- **Tire Pressure:** Check tire pressure monthly. Golf cart tires often run in the 15-25 PSI range (it's usually printed on the tire). Proper pressure ensures even tire wear and better range (for electric) or efficiency (for gas). Low pressure will give a softer ride but can risk wheel damage if you hit a bump hard, and high pressure rolls easier but can give a bumpier ride. Keep them even left to right to avoid pulling.

- **Tire Wear:** Rotate tires front-to-back occasionally if wear is uneven (fronts often wear differently, especially if alignment is off). Cupped or uneven wear might indicate an alignment issue.
- **Brake Adjustment:** Most carts have mechanical drum brakes on the rear. They often self-adjust, but sometimes you may need to adjust the brake cables or linkages if the pedal is getting too much travel. At least annually, inspect the brake shoes. It's not a bad idea to pull the drums and look at the shoes every couple years (particularly if you hear squeaking or the braking performance diminishes). Replace shoes as needed.
- **Brake Cables:** Ensure the brake cables (from pedal to drums) are not frayed and move smoothly. A little lubrication of the cable (or replacement if sticking) can keep brakes working nicely. If your cart has regenerative braking (like an RXV electric), less to maintain there on the motor brake, but still ensure any mechanical parking brake is functional.

Steering and Suspension:
- **Steering:** Grease any fittings (zerks) on the front end (some carts have grease points on

the kingpins or steering linkage). If the steering feels loose, check tie rod ends for play, and the steering rack for any issues. Tighten any loose bolts. Minor play can often be adjusted out via steering rack adjustments if specified by the manufacturer.
- **Suspension:** Check that leaf spring bushings are present and not overly worn. If the cart leans to one side, a spring might be sagging. Shocks (if present) should be checked for leaks. Replacing shocks or springs might be needed after many years, especially if the cart carries heavy loads often or has a rear seat (heavy-duty springs in the rear are common upgrades when a rear seat is added).
- **Wheel Bearings:** Rarely an issue unless the cart is very old, but listen for any grinding or wobble at the wheels. Repacking or replacing wheel bearings could be needed after a decade or more.

Annual or Seasonal Maintenance Checklist:

Here's a quick checklist that owners can perform (modify based on usage – heavy use might require more frequent checks):

- **Every Use or Weekly:**

- Electric: plug in to charge; quick visual of batteries.
- Gas: check fuel level; listen for any odd sounds.
- Tires: glance for any flats or low pressure.
- **Monthly:**
  - Check tire pressure with a gauge; inflate as needed.
  - Check battery water levels (if lead-acid).
  - Do a slow test of brakes in a safe area to ensure they're grabbing well.
- **Every 3-6 Months:**
  - Clean batteries and terminals.
  - Grease any fittings (front end, pedal pivot, etc., if present).
  - Inspect brake cables and wiring for any wear or damage.
  - Look over tires for embedded nails, etc.
- **Yearly (or Biannually if light use):**
  - Electric: Clean battery compartment thoroughly. Load test batteries (optional).
  - Gas: Change engine oil and filter; clean air filter or replace; new spark plug.

- Remove wheels and inspect brakes; clean brake drums.
- Inspect suspension and steering components for wear.
- Do a thorough cleaning of the cart, touch up any rust spots on a steel frame with paint.
- If applicable, service the differential (some have oil that might need changing every few years).
- Check all lights and electrical accessories.
- For both: If stored, prepare (stabilize fuel or charge batteries fully).

Many owners find that their yearly maintenance costs are quite low – maybe the cost of oil and a spark plug for gas, or distilled water and baking soda for electric, plus any little fixes. However, big ticket items like battery replacement or a new set of tires will come up every so often, so budget for those in the long term.

Common Issues and Tips:
- If an electric cart won't go, common culprits are: a tripped circuit breaker or blown fuse, a bad solenoid (clicking but not engaging), or dead batteries. Often, something simple like a loose wire on the solenoid or corrosion can

cause loss of power. Keeping connections clean and tight prevents many problems.
- If a gas cart won't start or runs rough: check basics – fuel, spark, air. A clogged carburetor jet from old gas is routine – using fuel stabilizer and occasionally some carb cleaner can help. Also, gas carts have micro-switches for the pedal (to start/stop the engine when you press the gas) – those can fail over time, leading to no cranking.
- Squeaky suspension or steering: usually indicates some dry bushing – a little silicone spray or grease can do wonders. For older carts, a bushing kit (cheap) can tighten things up.
- Reduced range (electric): aside from batteries aging, check for dragging brakes (jack up the wheels and spin them to see if brakes are too tight) or under-inflated tires, as those increase rolling resistance.
- Lighting issues: If lights dim or blow out on an electric cart, ensure you have a proper **voltage reducer** (converts 36/48V to 12V). All accessories should run off 12V, either from a reducer or a dedicated 12V aux battery, not directly off part of the battery pack (which causes uneven battery wear).
- Strange noises: Clicking from the rear on a turn could be an issue with the differential or

axle splines – not common but can occur. Whining from an electric motor could indicate worn motor bearings.

Staying on top of maintenance not only prevents breakdowns but also retains your cart's value. If you keep records of service (even just a log of dates and what you did), it will impress a future buyer and show that the cart was cared for.

Now that we've covered how to maintain the cart, let's talk money. In Chapter 12, we will discuss **operating costs and budgeting** for owning a golf cart – including electricity vs gas costs, typical maintenance expenses, and even tips on financing or saving money in the long run.

Chapter 12: Operating Costs and Budgeting for Ownership

OWNING A GOLF CART is generally affordable, especially compared to a car, but it's wise to understand the ongoing costs. Prospective buyers should consider not just the purchase price, but also the expenses of using and maintaining the cart. In this chapter, we'll break down the typical costs of owning a golf cart – from energy/fuel and maintenance to insurance and potential upgrades – and provide some budgeting tips. We'll also touch on financing options for the initial purchase if you're buying new or high-end.

Electricity vs Gasoline Costs:
One of the biggest day-to-day costs is what it takes to run the cart. Electric carts need charging; gas carts need fuel. Let's estimate:

- *Electricity:* Suppose you have a 48V electric cart with, say, a 150 Ah battery pack (which is 7.2 kWh of energy if fully discharged, since 48V x 150Ah = 7200 Wh, or 7.2 kWh). In reality, you won't use all of that in a day unless you drive a lot. But let's say you consume 5 kWh on a day of use (that might be a couple rounds of golf or several miles of driving). If electricity is $0.12 per kWh (national average-ish), that's $0.60 to recharge – basically under a dollar a day for quite heavy use. Even if electricity is $0.20/kWh, 5 kWh is $1.00. So, in many cases, **charging a golf cart might only be a few dollars per month** – it's negligible for most people's budgets. It may be a bit more if you use it constantly (e.g., security patrol using 10 kWh a day, but that's a lot). For perspective, some sources note that by virtually every measure, electric carts are cheaper to operate than gas – no fuel to buy, and minimal maintenance.
- *Gasoline:* Gas carts have small engines, but they can still consume fuel. If a gas cart gets maybe around 20-30 mpg equivalent (just an estimate, they're not rated like cars, but some owners report using about 5 gallons for 100 or so miles). Gas prices vary; at $3 per gallon, driving 100 miles might cost $15. If you only

drive 10 miles a week (which could be typical for community use), that's about 40 miles a month, roughly 2 gallons, about $6 a month. If you drive a lot more, say 200 miles a month, maybe $30 in fuel. So, gas might be on the order of a few to several dollars a month for modest use. It's higher than electric, but still not huge absolute numbers unless you're putting lots of hours on it. Where gas can get pricier is if you do long days of use (like 8 hours a day on a farm – then you might be refilling more often). Still, compared to a car or even an ATV, a golf cart sips fuel by comparison.

Maintenance and Repairs Budget:

We covered tasks in the last chapter – here's how they translate to costs:

- *Routine Maintenance:* Oil, filters, spark plug for gas – maybe $20-30 a year if you do it yourself. Air filter maybe $10. For electric, distilled water $5 and some baking soda for cleaning, negligible cost. So annual routine stuff is cheap.
- *Battery Replacement:* This is the big one for electric. Suppose a set of new batteries is $800 and they last 5 years – that's $160/year on average. If they last 6 years, ~$133/year.

If you upgrade to lithium, say $2500 upfront but last 10 years – $250/year. It's wise to set aside a little each year toward the future battery fund. Some people proactively start saving for new batteries from day one.

- *Tires:* Golf cart tires can last a long time (many years) since speeds are low and many are on soft turf or smooth pavement. But eventually (maybe 5+ years or if you use it a lot on roads, the tread wears), a new set of 4 tires might be $200-$400 depending on type (installed). That's maybe $40-80 a year if amortized. If you have fancier wheels, just tires can be changed.
- *Brakes:* Replacement brake shoes might be $50 for parts and should last many years. Cables maybe $30 each if needed. These are infrequent expenses, maybe every 5-10 years you might overhaul brakes if usage is heavy.
- *Misc. Repairs:* Things like a solenoid ($30-$50), a controller ($300-$600), an engine carburetor cleaning or rebuild ($50-$100), etc., might crop up. It's not common for major parts to fail in early years, but as a cart ages, you might have a random $100-200 fix occasionally. Budget maybe $100/year for unexpected bits (this is a guess; some years $0, another year $300 for a new motor bearing or such).

- *Accessories and Upgrades:* If you plan to customize, include that in your budget. It's easy to spend a few hundred here and there on lights, seats, etc. This is optional, of course.

Insurance Costs:

Golf cart insurance, if you need it, can vary. Some insurers offer it as an add-on to homeowner's policy for maybe $50/year (liability only). A fuller coverage might be $100-$150/year or more, depending on your location and coverage. Progressive, for example, notes that golf cart insurance is customizable and likely cheaper than auto. Compared to car insurance (which can be hundreds per year), golf cart insurance is usually quite affordable – often under $200 annually for a good policy. Still, include it. If you are bundling with home/auto, you might get a discount.

Registration and Taxes:

If you register the cart as an LSV, you may have to pay registration fees. Often these are lower than car registration, but it could be, say, $30-$100 per year depending on state. Some states might also require property tax or vehicle tax on it (some treat it like a vehicle, others might not). For example, in some counties you might see a small personal property tax bill yearly like you do for cars or boats. It's usually minimal given the value (unless it's a fancy cart worth a lot). If you're just using it privately, no registration costs except maybe a one-time local permit if applicable.

Storage and Charging Infrastructure:

Do you need any special setup? Many people keep their cart in a garage or shed. If you don't have space, consider that you may need a small enclosure or rent a storage spot (some communities have cart barns or storage for a fee). Most of the time you can just park it at home at no extra cost. Charging simply uses a regular outlet, but make sure you have an outlet accessible. If not, maybe an electrician might install one where you need (one-time cost). If you live in an upstairs condo with no outlet in parking, that's a challenge – you'd need to find a solution for charging (this could be a limitation that influences your ability to own one).

Financing the Purchase:

If you are buying a new cart or a high-end used one, you might finance it rather than pay cash. Many dealers offer financing plans. For example, some manufacturers have promotions like 0% for 24 months or low interest for certain terms, especially during off-peak seasons. The monthly payment on a

$8,000 cart financed for 3 years at, say, 5% interest would be about $240 a month. For budgeting, you'd consider that alongside maybe insurance and such. If you go used, typically private sellers want cash. You could potentially use a personal loan if needed, but interest rates might be higher. Some people also finance via credit unions or specialty lenders. Given the relatively lower cost, many do pay outright, but financing is there if spreading out the cost is helpful. Just don't forget to factor interest into the total cost.

Resale and Depreciation (Long-Term Cost):

While you spend money on a cart, remember you can get some back when you sell it (unless you run it into the ground). Depreciation on carts tends to be slower than cars. If you buy a new cart for $10k, it might be worth maybe $6-7k in 3 years (losing ~$1k/yr in value), then maybe $5k in 5-6 years, and then it might hold around that until batteries die, etc. So depreciation is a cost (especially if new). Used carts might depreciate even less per year if bought at a fair price. Some well-kept used carts essentially cost very little over a few years of ownership – you might buy at $4k and sell at $3.5k three years later, effectively "spending" only $500 plus maintenance and such. So if you take care of it, the *net* cost of ownership (purchase minus resale) can be very reasonable.

Summarizing Typical Annual Costs: (These will vary widely, but as an example for moderate use)

- Electricity: $50 (maybe generous; likely less).
- Gas (if gas model): $100-$150 (instead of electricity).
- Maintenance: $100 (assuming minor stuff, averaging in tires/batteries over life).
- Insurance: $100.
- Registration: $50. That sums to maybe a few hundred per year, not counting any loan payment. With a loan, add your annualized cost of that.

One source pointed out that **yearly maintenance costs** (wheel alignment, oil changes, tire rotations, etc.) can range from about $500 to $2000 – however, that higher end likely includes significant repairs or a scenario with less DIY. If you maintain yourself and the cart is in good shape, it should be on the lower side. The same source noted **battery replacement $800 to $2,500** and battery life 3-10 years, which we've covered. So budgeting for those eventual costs is prudent.

Saving Money Tips:

- **Do It Yourself:** Most golf cart maintenance tasks are DIY-friendly. Learning to do basic things can save a lot on labor costs.
- **Off-Season Deals:** If you're buying a cart or parts, prices can sometimes be better in the fall/winter when demand is lower. Also, some dealers clear out inventory or demo units at a discount.
- **Used Parts/Accessories:** The golf cart community is big, and often people upgrade, leaving good used stock parts available. If you need a replacement motor or a body part, you might find one used for much less than new. Just ensure it's in good condition.
- **Efficient Usage:** For electric carts, follow good charging practices to prolong battery life (saves money by extending replacement interval). For gas carts, don't let them idle unnecessarily (most automatically stop when not moving, which is good).
- **Bundle Purchases:** If buying new, negotiate – sometimes dealers might throw in free accessories (like a windshield or upgraded wheels) or a year of free maintenance.
- **Insurance bundling:** as mentioned, adding to your home policy might be cheaper than a standalone policy.

Environmental and Long-Term:

One cost often overlooked is environmental impact – while not directly hitting your wallet immediately, it's worth noting: Electric carts produce no local emissions, which is great (though disposing of lead-acid batteries has an environmental cost; however, they are recycled in high percentages in the battery industry). Gas carts emit carbon monoxide and pollutants and consume fossil fuel. Some communities factor this in by encouraging electric carts only, which in the long run might also affect resale (electric could be in more demand). If gas prices spike, the cost difference could also widen.

In conclusion, **owning a golf cart can be very budget-friendly**, especially when compared to car ownership or other hobbies like boating or off-roading. With a few hundred dollars a year, you can keep a cart in great running shape. Just plan for those periodic larger expenses (tires, batteries) so they don't catch you off guard. Many people find that the convenience and fun a golf cart provides far outweighs the relatively low costs of ownership.

As we near the end of our handbook, we've covered almost everything from pre-purchase considerations to maintenance and costs. In the next chapter, we'll provide a handy **buying process checklist** to walk you through the steps of actually purchasing your cart, and ensure you don't miss any important steps.

Then we'll wrap up with a conclusion and a look at future trends in the golf cart world.

Chapter 13:
The Buying Process – Step-by-Step and Checklist

YOU'VE DONE YOUR homework – now it's time to actually buy a golf cart! This chapter is all about execution. We'll guide you through a suggested **step-by-step process** for buying your cart and provide a comprehensive **checklist** (especially useful if you're buying a used cart). The goal is to make sure you cover all bases, ask the right questions, and end up satisfied with your purchase.

Step 1: Define Your Requirements and Budget

Before you even contact sellers or visit dealers, clearly outline what you want:

- Gas or electric?
- New or used (and if used, how old is acceptable)?

- How many seats?
- Any "must-have" features (e.g., street-legal setup, or needs to fit in a certain space, or has to climb a steep hill to your house)?
- Budget limit (for purchase, separate from future upgrades).

Having this written down prevents impulse decisions. It's easy to get swayed by a shiny custom cart that might not actually fit your initial needs.

Step 2: Research What's Available

Use the internet, local ads, and dealer visits to see what's out there. If new, compare quotes from a couple of dealers if possible. If used, scan listings for a few weeks to learn the market prices. Knowledge is power: you'll recognize a good deal (or a rip-off) better when you've seen many examples. Also, research the sellers – if a dealer, check reviews; if an individual, maybe see if they are active in a community (some trust can be built if you know they're a local member of a club, etc.).

Step 3: Contact Seller and Ask Preliminary Questions

If you find a listing for a used cart (or even when talking to a dealer about a specific used unit), ask initial questions:

- How old is the cart (model year)?
- If electric: how old are the batteries?
- Any modifications or non-stock parts?
- Does it have a clean ownership (any liens, etc., usually not applicable unless financed)?
- Why are they selling? (Gives insight; e.g., upgrading to new one, or no longer need it).
- For dealers: was it a rental or trade-in? Any refurbishment done?

Gauge their responses. A knowledgeable, honest seller will give details. Vagueness or defensiveness is a red flag. For instance, if a seller can't tell you the year or says "I think batteries are fine, not sure when changed", then you know you must inspect closely.

Step 4: In-Person Inspection and Test Drive

Never buy sight-unseen (unless it's new from dealer with warranty). When you meet, take your time to go over the cart. Use the following **checklist** during inspection (feel free to have this printed out):

Visual/Physical Inspection:

- **Batteries (if electric):** Check each battery for bulging (bad sign), corrosion on terminals, proper water level. Note the brand and date codes if visible (some have a sticker

like "E-18" meaning May 2018, etc.). Ask to see the charger and verify it works.
- **Engine (if gas):** Check oil level and look/smell the oil (not sludgy or gasoline-smelling ideally). Look at the air filter. Any oil leaks underneath? A quick peek at the spark plug condition if possible.
- **Frame:** Look under the cart at the frame for any rust, cracks, or welds. Surface rust on an older steel frame can be okay if minor, but heavy rust or repaired breaks are concerning.
- **Wiring:** Are the wires neatly routed and in good condition? Messy wiring with lots of electrical tape could mean DIY add-ons that might be problematic. If there are extra accessories, ensure they didn't just twist wires into the battery (should have a proper reducer or separate 12V source).
- **Tires:** Note tire condition and tread. All four matching? Any dry rot (cracks in sidewall)? Also check that the rims aren't bent.
- **Suspension & Steering:** Push the cart side to side and up and down. Does anything clunk? Look at the tie rods and kingpins as someone gently moves steering back and forth (ignition off, of course) – excessive play?

- **Brakes:** In park, press the brake – does it feel firm or go to floor? Test the parking brake locks and releases smoothly.
- **Exterior:** Walk around – any cracks in the body? (Not a deal killer, but cosmetic). Are seats torn? Roof intact? Windshield clear?
- **Accessories:** Confirm all included accessories work – lights (have seller press brake and see brake lights, test blinkers, etc.), horn honks, radio plays, etc. If street-legal kit installed, make sure it's all functional.

Test Drive:

- **Starting:** Does it start up easily? Electric: key on and go (no hesitations, solenoid click should be heard then smooth takeoff). Gas: does it crank quickly and start within a second or two of pressing pedal? Listen for any unhealthy sounds during startup.
- **Acceleration:** Does it accelerate smoothly? Any jerking or stuttering (could indicate controller or carb issues)? Electric should be almost silent except maybe a whir; gas will have engine noise – make sure it's not backfiring or sputtering.
- **Top Speed:** If possible in a safe area, get it to top speed. Does it reach expected speed? (It's good to know roughly what it should do; if it

feels too slow, maybe the governor is very tight or batteries weak).
- **Braking:** Does it stop in a straight line and firmly? Any squeals (some brake noise can be normal if carts sat long)? If it has regen braking (like some electrics), does that function (cart slows itself when foot off throttle)?
- **Handling:** Turn in both directions fully – feel for any binding or odd clunks. Carts have limited suspension, but it should feel stable and predictable. On a lift, a bit more body roll is normal.
- **Hill Test:** If possible, climb a slope or hill with it. Electric: note if it slows excessively (batteries/motor issue) or handles it fine. Gas: should climb steadily without stalling. If it's a minor hill and the cart barely goes up, something's off.
- **Reverse:** Test reverse gear – electric: does it beep and move back smoothly? Gas: shifts into reverse and goes back (some slight gear grinding when shifting gears in some gas carts can happen if engine isn't fully stopped – but chronic grinding is not good).
- **Noises:** Listen throughout – any clicking, grinding, excessive vibration? Electric carts might have a slight electrical hum or brake click; gas will have engine vibrations but

shouldn't have knocking or anything alarming.
- **Odors:** Do you smell anything weird? Burning smells could mean a dragging brake or electrical short. Gas smell could indicate fuel leak or carb overflow.

After test driving, if it's a used private sale, now is time to review any **documentation**:

- Ask for maintenance records or receipts (especially for expensive things like a new battery set or a recent engine rebuild).
- If street legal, ensure they have the title or registration paper ready to sign over.
- If still under any warranty (manufacturer or extended), see the paperwork.

Also, have a list of **questions to ask the seller** (some we did earlier, but a few more now that you've seen it):

- How often did you service it and what did you do?
- Ever had to replace the motor or controller? (For electric) / Ever rebuilt the engine or clutches? (For gas).
- Has it ever been in an accident or rolled over?
- If used off-road or on beach, any issues with water/salt exposure?

- For electric: do all the batteries charge evenly? (If they have a voltmeter, check each battery's voltage after charge – advanced step, but could reveal a weak one).

It can be helpful to **bring a friend** along as an extra set of eyes and ears (and for safety when meeting a stranger from online). They might catch something you miss.

Step 5: Negotiation and Purchase

If everything checks out and you want the cart, it's time to negotiate the price (if used). Do your negotiation respectfully, based on facts: e.g., "I like the cart, but I notice the tires are going to need replacement and the batteries are 4 years old. Considering that, would you accept $X?" Having cash in hand (or a means to pay immediately) gives you leverage. If the price is fair and the seller is firm, you must decide if you're willing to pay it or walk away. Remember, there are other carts out there, but if it's the perfect one, a small difference shouldn't derail it.

If buying from a dealer, there might be less wiggle room on price (especially on new carts with set MSRPs). But dealers can often throw in free accessories or a better warranty term rather than a big price cut. Don't hesitate to ask, "Could you include a free first service? Or perhaps a spare tire?" The worst they can say is no.

Ensure you clarify everything that comes with the cart:

- The charger (and any charging cords).
- Any accessories you discussed.
- If street legal, the title and any keys for locks, etc.
- If it has a winter cover or extra set of wheels as advertised, grab them.

For private sales, fill out a **Bill of Sale**. Include: date, price, names and addresses of buyer/seller, the cart's serial number (and make/model/year), and both sign it. This is your legal proof of purchase. If there's a title, sign that over according to your state rules (might need a notary in some states).

Step 6: After Purchase – Initial Tasks

Congrats, you are a golf cart owner! A few things to do immediately after purchase:

- If you trailer it home, make sure it's secured properly on the trailer (heavy carts can roll, always use wheel blocks or straps).
- When home, if used, consider doing a baseline maintenance: e.g., fully charge batteries and maybe do an equalization

charge if needed, or change the oil in a gas cart so you know the schedule fresh. This sets a starting point.
- If you need to register it (LSV), gather documents and head to DMV soon to handle that.
- Get insurance set up before driving on road.
- Read the owner's manual (if provided, or find it online) – there are often specific maintenance tips or operation notes.
- And of course, take it for a celebratory spin around your area (legally)!

Checklist – Questions to Keep in Your Pocket:

It can be overwhelming to remember everything, so here's a quick **question checklist** to use when talking to a seller (some were mentioned earlier, but compiled):

- How old is the cart (model year)? Any idea of usage history (course fleet, private owner, etc.)?
- How old are the batteries? When were they last replaced?
- If gas, has the engine ever been rebuilt or had major repairs?

- How was the cart primarily used and how often?
- What's the approximate mileage or hours on the cart (if it has an hour meter or if seller can estimate usage)?
- Is there any warranty left, or is it sold as-is?
- Any modifications or aftermarket parts installed? (Lift kit, controller, etc.)
- Have any repairs been made recently? (e.g., new brakes, new charger, etc.)
- Ever been in an accident or rolled?
- (If applicable) Does it come with a title and registration for street use?
- Are there any accessories included (covers, mirrors, etc.)?

This list, along with the inspection checklist, will ensure you get all the info you need. A well-informed buyer can negotiate a fair price and avoid hidden issues.

Final Thought in Buying Process: Don't rush. Unless you have a time crunch, it pays to be patient to find the right cart. There are lots of carts out there, and new ones coming onto the market especially as seasons change or leases end. By following a structured process, you greatly increase the odds that you'll end up with a golf cart that brings you joy and not headaches.

Now that you're presumably at the end of the journey (perhaps with a new golf cart in your garage!), we'll conclude this handbook in the next chapter with some final thoughts, tips for enjoying your golf cart, and a brief look at what the future might hold for golf cart enthusiasts.

Chapter 14: Conclusion and Future Trends

CONGRATULATIONS ON MAKING IT through *The Essential Golf Cart Buyer's Handbook*! By now, you should feel empowered with knowledge to make a wise purchase and to get the most out of your golf cart ownership experience. In this concluding chapter, we'll summarize key takeaways, offer some final tips for being a responsible and happy golf cart owner, and peek at where the world of golf carts is heading in the future.

Key Takeaways:
- **Know Your Needs:** Always circle back to how *you* plan to use the cart. The best cart is the one that fits your lifestyle – whether it's a simple two-seater for golf rounds or a tricked-out six-seater for family beach trips.
- **Do Your Research:** From understanding gas vs electric, to learning maintenance, to

checking local laws – doing homework pays off. It saves money, prevents buyer's remorse, and ensures safety.
- **Budget Beyond Purchase:** Remember that owning a cart involves some ongoing costs (though thankfully, quite manageable). Plan for those, especially battery replacements for electrics or eventual upgrades you might want.
- **Inspect Before You Buy:** We provided checklists for a reason – a careful inspection will save you from many common pitfalls like buying a cart with weak batteries or hidden damage. Don't hesitate to get a second opinion or even a professional inspection for expensive purchases.
- **Maintenance is Key:** A golf cart doesn't demand a lot, but regular maintenance – keeping batteries watered, changing oil, tightening bolts – will make your cart reliable and extend its life. As one expert insight highlighted, failing to perform routine maintenance can decrease performance and value over time.
- **Safety and Legal Compliance:** Always operate your cart responsibly. Follow the rules of your community or local traffic laws. Ensure if it's on public roads that it's properly equipped and insured. It's easy to have fun

safely if you take a few precautions (like using seat belts, not overloading passengers, etc.).
- **Enjoy and Engage:** One of the best parts of golf cart ownership is the community around it. Many neighborhoods have golf cart clubs or meetups. Parades of decorated golf carts happen in some towns during holidays. Don't be afraid to wave at fellow cart owners, share tips, or join online forums for your cart brand or area.

Future Trends in Golf Carts: The world of golf carts is not standing still. Here are a few trends and developments on the horizon:

- **Electric Dominance and Lithium Tech:** Electric carts are becoming the norm, not just for golf courses but also for personal transportation. With improvements in lithium battery technology, we can expect future carts to have longer range, shorter charge times, and even solar charging options. Some companies are already offering rooftop solar panels that can trickle charge batteries – the "solar golf cart" idea to extend range on sunny days.
- **Smart Features:** Just as cars are getting smarter, so are carts. We may see more integration of digital displays, GPS, and

Bluetooth connectivity. Imagine your cart having a built-in screen showing your golf course GPS and scorecard, or a backup camera for parking in your garage. Some high-end carts (like Garia) already have touchscreens and other techy features.

- **Eco-Friendly Communities:** The rise of *"Golf Cart Communities"* – neighborhoods or towns designed with golf cart travel in mind – is a trend. There are well-known retiree communities (e.g., The Villages in Florida) where carts are almost more common than cars, and even urban developments encouraging NEVs for short trips as a green initiative. This means infrastructure like dedicated cart lanes, special parking areas, and charging stations might become more common.
- **Street-Legal Expansion:** Regulations might become more standardized or relaxed to allow LSVs in more places as cities look to reduce car traffic. We might see more consistency in how states treat golf carts, possibly making it easier to register them. Conversely, safety standards could get stricter (for example, requiring carts to have certain stability features if they go on road).
- **Design and Comfort:** The aesthetics of carts are evolving. Modern designs like the Club

Car CRU or Yamaha concepts show futuristic looks, multi-use functionality (somewhere between a cart and a small car). Expect more comfortable seating, better suspensions for comfort, and even weather protection (some carts might come with integrated weather enclosures or even air conditioning – there are already some aftermarket A/C units for carts!).

- **Autonomy and Rentals:** It might be a while, but there's even experimentation with self-driving golf carts (for resorts or gated areas). On a simpler note, app-based rental golf carts (like scooter or bike shares) could become a thing in resort towns or large campuses, where you can rent a cart by the hour through your phone.
- **New Players and Competition:** With the surge in interest for small EVs, more companies may enter the market, possibly even automotive companies making "neighborhood vehicle" spinoffs. Competition usually brings better features and prices for consumers.

Despite all the innovation, the core appeal of golf carts will remain: a convenient, enjoyable way to get around for short distances, to enjoy the outdoors, and to make daily tasks a bit more fun. Whether you're an avid golfer, a beach town cruiser, or just someone who likes tinkering with small vehicles, a golf cart opens up a world of utility and leisure.

Final Tips for an Enjoyable Golf Cart Experience:

- Personalize it: Give your cart a name, a theme, or a little quirk that makes it feel like yours. It could be a custom decal or just a fun nickname.
- Include family/friends: If you have kids or grandkids, involve them (teach them safety too). A golf cart can be a family bonding tool – evening rides to get ice cream, etc.
- Keep it Secure: Unfortunately, carts can be a target for theft in some places. Consider a steering wheel lock or a hidden kill switch if that's a concern. Always take the keys out (seems obvious, but easy to forget when you're used to leaving it like a parked golf cart on a course).
- Document Your Adventures: Some people decorate their carts for holidays (4th of July parades, Christmas light tours). Take photos, join local events – you'll create great memories.
- Stay Informed: Keep this handbook handy as a reference, and update yourself with new

info. Subscribe to a golf cart magazine or forum if you become an enthusiast – there's always something new to learn or a cool mod to see.

At the end of the day, owning a golf cart is about enhancing your lifestyle – whether it simplifies chores or amplifies fun. We hope this handbook has armed you with all the essential knowledge and insider tips to buy confidently and enjoy thoroughly.

Thank you for reading *The Essential Golf Cart Buyer's Handbook*. Now, it's time to turn the page from reading to doing – go out there, find that perfect cart, and **enjoy the ride**!

About the Author

H.S. Collins has over 50 years in and around the golf cart industry with experience in service, sales and finance. He has personally sold hundreds of golf carts and been on the cutting edges of changes in the golf cart business.

Collins was a local Senior Club Champion golfer and enjoyed Airsoft until recently. H.S. Collins has written this book for his 16-year-old grandson as the two of them are partners in a golf cart accessory business. Their latest product is a Collapsible Utility Bed (C.U.D.) which you can check out at www.gccub.com.

www.ingramcontent.com/pod-product-compliance
Lightning Source LLC
Chambersburg PA
CBHW050649160426
43194CB00010B/1865